The Natural Alien

Humankind and Environment

The Natural Alien

Neil Evernden

Second Edition

UNIVERSITY OF TORONTO PRESS

Toronto Buffalo London

© University of Toronto Press Incorporated 1985, 1993
Toronto Buffalo London
Printed in Canada
Reprinted 1999

ISBN 0-8020-2962-0 (cloth)
ISBN 0-8020-7785-4 (paper)

Printed on acid-free paper

Canadian Cataloguing in Publication Data

Evernden, Lorne Leslie Neil
 The natural alien

 2nd ed.
 Includes index.
 ISBN 0-8020-2962-0 (bound) ISBN 0-8020-7785-4 (pbk.)

 1. Philosophical anthropology. 2. Man – Influence
 of environment. I. Title

 GF80.E94 1993   128   C93-093066-5

The first edition was published with
the help of a grant from the
Canadian Federation for the Humanities,
using funds provided by the
Social Sciences and Humanities
Research Council of Canada, and
a grant to the University of Toronto Press
from the Andrew W. Mellon Foundation.

For Derek and Blake

Contents

Preface

It seems a courtesy at least to forewarn the reader that this book, although concerned with the phenomenon we refer to as environmentalism, is by no means a treatise on environmental ills and remedies. There are no frightening statistics or calls to action, and no exhortations about wise resource use. There is only an examination of the affairs of mind that make it so difficult to espouse the cause of the environment without resorting to subterfuge. In fact, even the term 'environmentalist' is used here in a slightly unusual sense, to designate not a class of activists but simply those who confess a concern for the non-human.

A second warning may also be necessary to forestall a 'territorial' response from the many specialists whose areas of expertise are infringed upon. It is undoubtedly irritating to see one's vocation dealt with in a perfunctory way, but this may be partially alleviated if I clarify my intentions. Lewis Mumford, arguably the dean of generalists, once commented that 'the generalist has a special office, that of bringing together widely separated fields, presently fenced in by specialists, into a larger common area, visible only from the air. Only by forfeiting the detail can the over-all pattern be seen, though once that pattern is visible new details, unseen even by most thorough and competent field workers ... may become visible.'[1] This may seem to suggest too lofty a role for the generalist, but at least it indicates the difference in intent which must be recognized at the outset. What is sought is pattern, not detail, similarities rather than disjunctions. And speculation, anathema to the careful scholar, is the adhesive that binds the pieces together.

What follows is a discussion of how we have tended to think about the world, and how else we might think about it. Environment is never isolated from belief, and a discussion of environmentalism is inevitably also an account of the relationship of mind to nature – what Paul Shepard once called 'the central problem of human ecology.'[2] Our perceptions and expectations of environment are inseparable from our moral commitment to particular beliefs and institutions. Mary Douglas observes:

Tribal peoples who worship their dead ancestors often explicitly recognize that each ancestor only exists in so far as cult is paid to him. When the cult stops, the ancestor has no more credibility. He fades away, unable to intervene, either to punish angrily, or to reward kindly. We should entertain the same insight about any given environment we know. It exists as a structure of meaningful distinctions.[3]

This essay is essentially about those 'meaningful distinctions' that give us an environment, and about the difficulties implicit in any attempt to defend it.

A portion of chapter 2 has previously been published in my article 'Beyond Ecology: Self, Place, and the Pathetic Fallacy,' *The North American Review*, 263 (Winter 1978), 16–20; and some material in chapter 4 has been discussed in 'Seeing and Being Seen: A Response to Susan Sontag's Essays on Photography,' *Soundings*, 68:1 (1985).

While writing may be a solitary pursuit, it is never accomplished in isolation. The influence of others is vital, and any writer is endebted to a considerable variety of people. In the present instance there is an obvious debt to a tolerant and supportive family, to stimulating colleagues like William Leiss and Miriam Wyman, and to Rik Davidson and Joan Bulger of the University of Toronto Press. But I must especially acknowledge the long-term influence of William Fuller and John Livingston, both of whom exhibit standards of scholarship and friendship that would surpass anyone's expectation. To these and to others unnamed, my thanks.

NE
Toronto, December 1984

Preface to the Second Edition

When I began writing *The Natural Alien* ten years ago, my intentions were simply these: to question why, despite the serious attention of dedicated people, our 'environmental crisis' seemed to defy resolution; to suggest that any answer to that question must recognize that the crisis is essentially a cultural phenomenon, not merely a technical one; to indicate that reflections from a diversity of disciplines can be relevant to the topic; to ask whether certain 'alternate voices' might already exist in western culture which could rephrase our conceptualization of the environmental crisis; and to urge a fundamental rethinking of our position rather than a continual refurbishing of old and tarnished 'solutions.' I don't think my intentions have changed significantly over the intervening years, but I have certainly profited from the comments of many readers in the interim. Those comments lead me to think one question that might have been added was 'what next?'

Yet to address that question poses a certain dilemma for me, since I have indicated that I am fearful of the hypocrisy inherent in calling for a different approach and then falling into the usual pattern of thinking exclusively in terms of 'problems' and 'solutions.' Or perhaps I should say in terms of 'issues' and solutions, recognizing an important distinction that John Livingston has made in his book *Arctic Oil*. He suggests that the environmental dilemma, as reflected in the daily newspaper headlines, is commonly perceived as a series of issues – oil spills, endangered species, ozone depletion, and so forth – and that we are so overwhelmed by these that we seldom look deeper. But issues, he says, are analogous to the tips of icebergs: they are simply the visible portion of a much larger entity, most of which lies beneath the surface, beyond our daily inspection. The submerged mass constitutes the fundamental 'problem,' that domain of unspoken assumptions which legitimates, indeed even demands, the behaviour which precipitates the state of affairs we designate as 'the environmental crisis.' And although I could not have articulated that distinction as clearly and elegantly as Living-ston, my intention was certainly to concentrate on 'problems' rather than on 'issues.' I suspect that my having done so accounts in some measure for the continued interest in the book, since it is addressed to the resilient roots of our dilemma rather than to the ephemeral foliage of media gossip. And it is also that focus which makes it so difficult for me to accommodate the inevitable question 'what next?'

I have, therefore, attempted to strike a compromise. I cannot pretend to know what we ought to do next, and I must remain sceptical of those who profess to do so. The most I can do is to attempt to illustrate the way attention to 'problems' might modify our proclivity to address 'issues' in terms of past solutions. That is, having attempted to indicate the serious limits which our tacit assumptions place on our ability to respond to the perceived crisis, I have proceeded, in a new epilogue, to suggest how awareness of those limits might help us rethink the 'solutions du jour' which the popular media serve up in remarkable proportions. That is not to suggest that we need be fatalistic about our situation, or that no action can be taken (remembering, of course, that restraint from certain behaviour is also a significant form of action). Instead, it is to suggest that if we bring our critical attention to bear on the daily rhetoric of conservation and development, we may both dis-courage the habitual reinvention of 'solutions' which simply exacerbate our dilemma, and encourage the articulation of genuinely novel responses.

We must begin, however, with the recognition that the source of the environmental crisis lies not without but within, not in industrial efflu-ent but in assumptions so casually held as to be virtually invisible. Oscar Wilde once asserted that art does not imitate life, life imitates art: we come to occupy the landscape we create. If so, our scarred habitat is not only of our doing, but of our imagining, and it will take a profound recreation of the social world to 'un-say' the environmental crisis and constitute a more benign alternative.

To Virgil Duff and Theresa Griffin, my thanks for seeing this second edition through at the University of Toronto Press.

NE
Toronto, October 1992

The Natural Alien

CHAPTER ONE

Talking about the Mountain

The Dilemma

It has become common in our time for a person or group to speak out when some portion of undiminished nature is threatened with modification or extinction. Of course, not everyone feels compelled to defend a mountain. But those who do, whom we commonly refer to as environmentalists, find it an awkward compulsion, for they must reconcile the conflicting tasks of being faithful to their subject and maintaining their credibility. In recent years it has become increasingly difficult to assume that one can be both accurate and easily understood. That is, the perils of facile explanation have become all too apparent, and there has been much soul-searching about the path the environmentalist should cleave to. For those who have not been privy to these debates, the next few pages may serve as a brief summary. But the central task of the chapters that follow is not so much descriptive as exploratory, and the first step must be an examination of the failure of the environmental movement to achieve its goals.

To many this may sound rather perverse, given the widespread perception that the environmental movement is making significant headway in modifying public policy. And by some measures the movement certainly seems successful. But few who have watched their hard-won gains evaporate when a new batch of politicians arrives on the scene can dare to feel complacent. There is no assurance that even such reforms as have occurred will long endure if economic indicators seem to point elsewhere.

To clarify the environmentalists' dilemma we must begin by examining what has actually been done in the movement's name. However, we immediately encounter an obstacle, for no two environmentalists are likely to concur in their statements of intent. Their goals, conscious or otherwise, may overlap very little except in reference to an object of concern called 'environment.' The most public variations on this theme include what we might call preservation, which speaks to the defence of wilderness; conservation, which is concerned with the wise use of resources in perpetuity; and perhaps a kind of pastoralism, which is associated with rustic lifestyles and a return to simpler pleasures. But these do not exhaust the use of the term by any means. Indeed, there is cause to wonder whether it is a useful or appropriate one at all. We shall have to consider this later, but at this stage we must, for convenience at least, come to some understanding of what is meant by 'environmentalism' that will facilitate discussion. While it may seem a very general trait, I would suggest that concern is a feature common to all the variations of environmental advocacy. Each group or individual is motivated by some form of consideration for environment and seeks to communicate a concern to the public. For some that concern is fairly pragmatic and utilitarian, while for others environment is an entity of intrinsic worth that must be maintained. This is a significant difference, but for the moment we may describe an environmentalist as one who experiences a sense of value in nature and is moved to assert the reality of his experience to others. It is these expressions of concern that give the impression of an exceedingly diverse social movement.

In Anglo-American literature there is ample evidence of concern for nature, and even a history of various styles of 'talking about the mountain.' Generally we regard earlier environmental advocates as being preoccupied with aesthetics and metaphysics. Mountains were uplifting, sublime, even just beautiful. Because their comments were personal, we think of these environmentalists as being concerned with subjective aspects of the relationship between man and environment. But in recent history the balance has shifted. Something happened in the late 1960s – or, rather, something that had been happening for a long time suddenly became highly visible after Earth Day (22 April 1970). Everyone began to pay lip service to the environmental movement, and the American president of the day declared the 1970s to be the 'decade of the environment.' Inevitably this public expression of interest engendered, in bureaucratic circles, a craving for experts. Now that a problem had been identified, there was a need for people who had the ability to find solutions. It was to the universities, citadels of expertise and scientific management, that the bureaucrats turned. And there, as if waiting for discovery, was an obscure biological special- ity called 'ecology,' which was to become a household word.

It is a source of irritation to some ecologists that their discipline, which they endeavour to make as scientific and objective as possible, has become linked in the public mind with a rag-tag collection of natural- ists, poets, small-scale farmers, and birdwatchers who constitute a visible part of the environmental movement. Their grievance has semantic roots, in that 'ecology' is now being used to connote something quite different from its academic namesake. But these ecologists are also dismayed at seeing their work lumped together with the pseudo-science of some back-to-the-land advocates or with the sentimental musings of what the media call 'the ecology movement.' The connection between these and ecology proper is, they would say, extremely tenuous.

Yet, to the general public it may be the biologists' activities that seem foreign to ecology. What, after all, does the behaviour of one-celled organisms in test tubes, or the presence of fossils in a bog, or the popula- tion dynamics of mice have to do with 'protecting the ecology?' Even in informed circles there is confusion about what constitutes a proper ecology. This became apparent some years ago when Theodore Ros- zak's *Where the Wasteland Ends* was enjoying wide circulation. In it the author savaged some of our most cherished societal assumptions and institutions and then announced that there was hope in the emergence of a new and subversive science called ecology.

Ecology has been called 'the subversive science' – and with good reason. Its sensibility – wholistic, receptive, trustful, largely non-tampering, deeply grounded in aesthetic intuition – is a radical deviation from traditional science. Ecology does not systematize by mathematical generalization or materialist reductionism, but by the almost sensuous intuiting of natural harmonies on the largest scale. Its patterns are not those of numbers, but of unity in process; its psychology borrows from Gestalt and is an awakening awareness of wholes greater than the sum of their parts.[1]

This image of ecology is very appealing and may be accepted un-critically by the layman. Ironically, however, the usefulness of ecology to the environmental movement has derived not from this idealized ver-sion of it but from a decidedly anti-mystical biological specialty which seems bent on contradicting Roszak's assessment. The professional ecologist tries to make his discipline adhere as closely as possible to the tenets of normal science, and thus to make it a respectable and persua-sive voice. In contrast to Roszak's ideal, contemporary ecology is highly reliant on statistical inference. Even a cursory glance through the literature would persuade the novice of the value of learning to compre-hend differential equations before tackling the science of ecology, and a look at the job advertisements would convince him of the importance of being able to call himself a quantitative ecologist. There may well be subversive insights emerging from ecology, but the discipline itself is precisely what Roszak claims it is not. And while the environmentalist may sympathize with Roszak's version, it is to the scientific one that he turns for authoritative support of his endeavour.

This is an interesting contradiction, and one that may be indicative of a tension within the environmental movement. But for the moment we need only take note of the existence of two different 'ecologies,' vying for attention. It may be that most environmental advocates take no no-tice of this conflict, intent as they are on speaking in defence of the inarticulate and on protecting that which they feel to be of inestimable value. The weapons they choose in their defence of nature are select-ed almost solely on grounds of expediency – which, given the environ-mentalists' long history of rearguard action, is quite understandable.

It is difficult to say just when environmental advocacy began, and with it the continuous battle between these conservative earth-defenders and the champions of progress. In his history of 'ecologies,' entitled *Nature's Economy*, Donald Worster begins in the eighteenth century. This seems a reasonable choice, even though discussions of the relation-ship between man and nature can be encountered at almost any stage in history.[2] However, we are probably most familiar with the battles of the nineteenth and twentieth centuries, particularly as expressed by prominent figures like Henry David Thoreau and John Muir. The accomplishments of individual environmentalists are often astonishing, given the financial and political power of their adversaries,[3] but, despite their occasional triumphs, they have been perpetual underdogs. And the most effective means of discrediting them has been to brand them as impractical and emotional – in contrast to their sober, rational critics, of course. The implication has been that there is no real foundation for their claims, or at least none beyond the pathetic minds of the nature-lovers themselves. How selfish they are, say their detractors, to try to deny the nation its rightful bounty, or to try to interfere with personal profit and industrial growth, just because they have a weakness for fuzzy animals and picturesque scenery. Given their derogatory image as effete and sentimental fools, it is understandable that environmentalists have pounced on any line of argument that cannot be dismissed as merely subjective. Even today, critics warn that '"wilderness," in the hands of environmentalists, has become an all-purpose tool for stopping economic activity' and that 'environmentalism is reminiscent of the German Romanticism of the nineteenth century.'[4] In light of this, the appearance of scientific ecology on the scene must have seemed providential. In no time quantitative pronouncements by experts like Paul Ehrlich, Barry Commoner, and Garrett Hardin were adopted as a new gospel, and respectful attention was finally paid by a frightened public.

Perhaps the first dramatic evidence of the usefulness of ecology came through the courageous efforts of Rachel Carson. Those who remember the furore surrounding the publication of *Silent Spring* in 1962 will recall the embarrassment of Carson's opponents when it became evident that she could not be dismissed easily. She had 'facts and figures,' emblems of respectability that had long been the property of the developer and the technocrat. Since Carson's work could not just be dismissed, some resorted to character assassination, and some even to intimidation (her publisher was threatened with loss of textbook sales); others were content to rely on counter-experts to allay the fears Carson had aroused. *Time*, probably a fairly good indicator of the establishment view, published a mixed review of the book. The magazine commented favourably on the author's intentions, but devoted most of its space to presenting the reassuring opinions of 'experts.' The article makes interesting reading now, for many of the so-called excesses of Rachel Carson are the commonplaces of today. At one point the *Time* writer assures us that, while some pesticides may be dangerous, many 'are roughly as harmless as DDT' which is now banned in most industrial countries. The article concludes, in the best tradition of environmentalist put-downs, by saying that 'many scientists sympathize with Miss Carson's love of wildlife, and even her mystical attachment to the balance of nature. But they fear that her emotional and inaccurate outburst in *Silent Spring* may do harm by alarming the nontechnical public, while doing no good for the things that she loves.'[5]

Heaven forbid that anyone alarm the 'nontechnical public.' Ordinarily, any reference to 'emotional and inaccurate outbursts' or to a 'mystical attachment to the balance of nature' would be enough to discredit an author. But Carson was not being inaccurate, and time has vindicated her. Even *Time* has. And the lesson was not lost on the environmentalists. Perhaps their adversaries could be challenged with their own weapons? If ecology could show how toxic materials are concentrated in food chains and thereby bring the chemical industry down a notch or two, what might it do if matched against strip miners or hydroelectric developers? Ecology has thus become very much the darling of the environmental movement, and is expected to produce a continuous stream of ammunition for use against runaway development.

Universities, hastening to cash in on the new popularity of environmentalism in general and ecology in particular, have begun to turn out graduates in such fields as 'ecological planning' and 'wilderness management.' The new technicians fit admirably into government bureaucracies, which can then claim to be 'taking action' to protect 'our precious natural resources' – all within the guidelines of 'sound economic practice,' of course. To some the high profile of resource management and the abundance of environmental impact assessments are proof that the environmental movement has come of age, that it has shed the shrill emotionalism of its youth and matured into a rational collaborator in the continuing quest for a managed earth.

Yet, somehow, it still does not seem right. There remains a nagging unease amid all this apparent progress. Almost unnoticed, the tents in the wilderness have grown into alpine villages and amusement centres. Enjoying the great outdoors has become a euphemism for playing with expensive toys: four-wheel-drive vehicles now frolic in places formerly protected by benign neglect, and snowmobiles terrorize winter. The most common element in the outdoor experience has become other people, a fact celebrated by many park users. Some professionals privately admit that the best way to destroy a natural area is to designate it a park. But even if this is less than the environmentalist had hoped for, there is a general optimism that improvements in management methodology will finally lead to a situation superior to anything that could have resulted from the old emotional environmentalism. Where once only an anguished cry could be expected in defence of a threatened mountain or an endangered species, now a detailed inventory and a benefit-cost analysis are sure to be forthcoming. The system will say all that needs to be said about the mountain – and say it with numbers.

This shift in tactics has constituted a change in emphasis as well, from the personal testimony of experienced value to an 'objective' elucidation of public interest. That is, while in the past the naturalist-orator tried to evoke in his listener a sensation reminiscent of his own in the presence of nature, it is now possible simply to show the man in the street what's in it for him. By excising emotion and concentrating on numbers the environmentalist can show even the disinterested that it is prudent, economic, to retain a particular mountain in its present state. And since economics in this broad sense is believed to be fundamental to everyone's well-being, what was formerly a minority concern becomes a cause for all. We must protect and/or wisely manage our natural resources, because if we do not we may compromise our standard of living. Through such arguments the new managerial form of environmental action attempts to accomplish what decades of inspired prose and rhetoric could not.

But something is lost or compromised in this change of emphasis. This much has been evident since the inception of resource management, as the tension between such men as John Muir and Gifford Pinchot illustrates. But even those who, ten years ago, might have been judged the spiritual descendants of Pinchot and his conservationists are today uneasy about their accomplishments. Men who once wrote books and articles advocating increased use of environmental impact assessments and park master plans have begun to caution against reliance on such devices. John Livingston's *The Fallacy of Wildlife Conservation* and David Ehrenfeld's *The Arrogance of Humanism* demonstrate this shift, and more are sure to follow as the fragility of environmental legislation becomes apparent. For, at bottom, nothing has really changed. The natural environment remains vulnerable whenever there are short-term benefits to be had by sacrificing environmental protection. The basic attitude towards the non-human has not even been challenged in the rush to embrace utilitarian conservation. By basing all arguments on enlightened self-interest the environmentalists have ensured their own failure whenever self-interest can be perceived as lying elsewhere.

Therein lies the fatal weakness of the so-called ecology movement. In seizing arguments that would sound persuasive even to indifferent observers environmentalists have come to adopt the strategy and assumptions of their opponents. As Anthony Brandt has observed, the industrialist and environmentalist tacitly agree on one thing: that nature is for something. Nature is a conglomeration of natural resources, a storehouse of materials. 'The industrialist and the environmentalist are brothers under the skin; they differ merely as to the best use the natural world ought to be put to.'[6] In their haste to persuade society of the significance of the non-human they have succumbed to the temptations of expediency. They have endorsed the search for subterfuges, for ways to encourage the behaviour they want, without having to contend with the attitudes embraced by the majority.

The Fatal Flaw

At one time it was common to encounter, as a filler in newspapers and magazines, reports that science had determined the current worth of the human body to be $12.98, or some such figure. This amount, determined by adding up the market value of the materials which make up the body, was thought to be amusing just because it was absurd. Everyone realizes that an actual, functioning human life is worth something quite different; to insist on treating only the material worth of the person is plainly outrageous. But at one time the environmentalist would have said the same thing about nature. Certainly, one can measure its composition and conclude that as a collection of natural resources it is worth a given amount of money. But to do this is vastly to underestimate, indeed completely to misunderstand, the kind of value experienced by a person in the presence of nature. The kind of evaluation permitted by our societal institutions is simply too narrow to accommo-

date the concerns of the environmentalist. Applying monetary evaluation to nature is dangerous to start with, just because it encourages a
comparison between the uses of each mountain. As soon as its worth is
greater as tin cans than as scenery, the case for the mountain vanishes.
But, more important, monetary evaluation distracts us from the fact
that the values at issue are not economic in the first place. It is all these
other values that are at risk when the environmentalist opts for the
argument from expediency.

In his analysis of the failure of wildlife conservation John Livingston minces no words in his description of current tactics. Environmental impact assessment is, he says, 'a grandiloquent fraud, a hoax,
and a con' because it gives the appearance of being for the benefit of
the environment while actually serving the interests of the developer.
'Ecology is thus used as a tool to permit "developers" to continue to do
what they have always done. The only difference is that "environmental
impact is to be minimized to an acceptable level." What is minimal
impact? What is acceptable impact? Acceptable to whom? Wildlife, alas,
cannot be interviewed.'[7]

Statements as blunt as Livingston's demonstrate the growing realization among environmentalists that they have, at least in one sense,
'sold out.' As we have seen, it is not particularly surprising that this
should happen. Who can blame them for seizing upon an approach
that seemed to achieve what years of honest witnessing had not? They
had tried telling society it was wrong, and no one listened. Now instead they are telling society it is stupid. Environmental degradation is
not necessarily wrong; it is just imprudent. This works – or at least it
gets attention. But the question society wants answered is not how to be
right, but how to be smart – how to go on doing what it has been
doing, without paying the price. And in offering to answer that question
the environmentalists have tacitly acknowledged the societal goals they
had initially challenged.

There is a simple illustration of the pressure towards compromise,
one every environmental sympathizer must have encountered. What do
you do when, after expressing support for some creature, the person
next to you demands: 'what good is it?' The spell is broken, for that
question reveals two different assumptions at work. The environmentalist has been assuming intrinsic value in the creature. The question

denies that, and asserts the assumption that human beings are the sole bearers and dispensers of value. The latter assumption, being ubiquitous, immediately predominates, and the advocate is on the defensive. He must come up with some use for that creature, something by which to justify its existence to the other person. Ehrenfeld refers to this as the 'humanists' trap.' '"Do you love Nature?" they ask. "Do you want to save it? Then tell us what it is good for." The only way out of this kind of trap, if there is a way, is to smash it, to reject it utterly.'[8] Perhaps the best the environmentalist can hope to do is to reply: 'what good are you?' – not to insult the other but to illustrate the absurdity of our presumption that one being's existence can be justified only by its utility to another. Otherwise, one risks succumbing to the humanists' trap, which is essentially the plight of modern environmentalism.

It is a strange phenomenon, this acceptance of impossible standards as a basis of environmental defence. What army would agree to let its opponent choose the ground and select the weapons? The stupidity of this acquiescence is even more apparent when we compare it with an analogous situation in which the bias is more obvious. Suppose your were a lawyer defending a client who happens to be black. What would you do if faced with a trial judge who denies your client any rights and who, after hearing your case, simply says: 'so what – is he white?' To the bigot your client can be conceived as worthy only if he is white. What should you do? Demand that the judge recognize the rights and dignity of your client, or detail his genealogical records at length to try to prove that he has white blood in his family tree? Essentially this is what the environmentalist does. When challenged to justify his declaration on behalf of the living world, he proceeds, not to oppose the assumptions of his critics, but to try 'to prove his client white.' Rather than challenge the astonishing assumption that only utility to industrialized society can justify the existence of anything on the planet, he tries to invent uses for everything, uses which Aldo Leopold recognized over thirty years ago as mere subterfuges to help defend the economically indefensible. Thoreau exposed the absurdity of this kind of assessment a century ago:

The legislature will preserve a bird professedly not because it is a beautiful creature, but because it is a good scavenger or the like. This, at least, is the defense set up. It is as if the question were whether some celebrated singer of the human race – some Jenny Lind or another – did more harm or good, should be destroyed, or not, and therefore a committee should be appointed, not to listen to her singing at all, but to examine the contents of her stomach and see if she devoured anything which was injurious to the farmers and gardeners, or which they cannot spare.[9]

And, naturally, such subterfuges ultimately fail, for some clients are not white and some creatures are not 'economic.' Over the long term the only defence that can conceivably succeed in the face of this prejudice is one based on the intrinsic worth of life, of human beings, of living beings, ultimately of Being itself.

Many would argue, however, that, when faced with a bigoted judge, a lawyer has no choice but to play by his rules (ignoring appeals to higher courts, etc). It may be good for the soul, they say, to challenge that judge's beliefs, but the client will surely wind up behind bars. And if, in fifty years or so, the defence argument is cited as helping to transform the attitudes of society and to prevent such judges sitting on the bench, the client will not be around to enjoy the victory. It is one thing to say that the environmentalist should not have to justify the existence of each creature in economic terms, but quite another to try to protect wildlife here and now, without using every argument available.

But even if the case for expediency is understandable, it is by no means obvious that the results justify it. A stay of execution is only as permanent as a government committee or a public-opinion poll. And in some instances the kind of preservation achieved may be only an illusion of victory. Some species are entrusted to zoos, for example, where their genes may continue to exist – if the customers keep coming. But an animal is not just genes. It is an interaction of genetic potential with environment and with conspecifics. A solitary gorilla in a zoo is not really a gorilla; it is a gorilla-shaped imitation of a social being which can only develop fully in a society of kindred beings. And that society in turn is only itself when it is in its environmental context, and so on. To attempt to preserve only a package of genes is to accept a very restricted definition of animality and to fall into the trap of mistaking the skin-encapsulated object for the process of relationships that constitutes the creature in question. To us, children of a society which finds objects more real than relationships or experience, this may seem a minor point. I hope it will cease to seem minor as our investigation proceeds.

Cutting the Vocal Cords

It is difficult to imagine the world as anything but a collection of objects, each amenable to study and control. A gorilla is, after all, *nothing but* the manifestation of a particular kind of DNA. And cattle are nothing but protein, and a mountain nothing but rocks and minerals. A tree is a cellulose support structure, a river is energy (going to waste unless dammed), and the human body is a collection of a few dollars worth of chemicals. We pride ourselves on our ability to get to the bottom of life's mysteries, that is, to reduce them to their basic components. The world is made up of parts, just like a car. And, knowing the nature of those parts and the way they are put together, man can not only understand but also control nature. The revelation of 'the way the world is'[10] is part of the hidden curriculum of the educational systems of the industrialized West. But it involves not so much the imparting of information as the insinuation of an article of faith.

However, our transformation from beings with an interest in mysteries and animate nature to beings with an interest in a mechanical order did not come easily or quickly, and still does not. Children are prone to assume that the world is, like themselves, alive and sensate. Only age and education can 'correct' their view. Indeed it would be no exaggeration to say that even graduate study at the university is a continuation of this corrective process. The attainment of objectivity entails a particular rite of passage, but one that occurs with surprisingly little fanfare. For our purposes the appropriate example is probably the education of the ecologist, although in fact any specialty would do as well. But ecology, and science in general, provides a distillate of the most significant tenets of our society and can help to illustrate the development of the impasse the environmentalist has reached.

As noted earlier, ecology aspires not to being a modern religion or secular value system but to being a science. Naturally, indoctrination into the ways of science must form a significant element in the education of the ecologist, although this is seldom spelled out in the prospectus.

The omission is not deliberate, but it is probably a fortunate one for those charged with recruiting new students. For it is unlikely that potential students, who by and large are people with a strong interest in, and possibly feeling for, animals and plants (or at least their experience of animals and plants) would be attracted by discussions of the philosophy of science. Not surprisingly, a common complaint from such students after they enter university is that they seldom encounter a living creature. The animal is replaced with abstractions.

The first stage of this process involves the placing of the living world into an academic context, and the labelling of all organisms with intellectually binding, tongue-defying nomenclature. Once the categories have been established and learned by rote, then a similar taxonomy is applied to all the parts of the beast-machine. To accomplish this the student must spend a couple of years cutting up bodies. By this time he or she will have begun to acquire the mental skills requisite to a scientific appraisal of organisms, and to realize that the object of science is theories, not animals.

Of course, vestiges of the initial impetus – the fascination with life – can persist well into graduate school. It is not uncommon to find students who claim to be 'working on' wolves (or rattlesnakes, or some other fabulous beast), which means that they will spend several years looking for some excuse for their passion, something that will eventually lead to a thesis. By contrast, the well-indoctrinated student will have realized that he is not studying animals at all, and that the hypothesis to be tested must be framed before he decides which creature to inflict it on. The goal is not observing animals but obtaining living material on which to test your theory.

The introduction to experimental physiology often marks the culmination of the undergraduate indoctrination. It is, in a sense, a test of the student's success in achieving the primary goal, which is something like the substitution of neutral matter for animate nature. If the student has become sufficiently detached, is suitably objective about animals, he will have no difficulty in mastering this final phase. If that has been accomplished, there will be no squeamishness about the blood that spurts out when these lives – the first the student has encountered in his university career – are put to the knife. And there will be no flinching if the animal screams (to be referred to hereafter as emitting 'high-pitched vocalization'[11]), since flinching can pull out catheters and otherwise disrupt a delicate dissection. And, of course, there should be no remorse when the animal is killed (or, as they say, is 'sacrificed' – perhaps a more accurate phrase than was intended). If the student has attained this level of detachment, he is ready to graduate and take his place in some industrial or governmental data-factory.

In reaching this goal the student has accomplished the ultimate act of the vivisectionist: he has severed the vocal cords of the world. This is a particularly significant image, but one which requires elaboration.

The study of experimental physiology became a major influence during the last century, although significant work was done even earlier. Claude Bernard, revered as the father of experimental medicine, published his classic *An Introduction to the Study of Experimental Medicine* in 1865. Bernard worked without anaesthetics and had to confine his subjects physically in order to operate. To his wife's horror, he would sometimes bring partially dismembered creatures home with him, so that he could observe their response to his handiwork. He described one such animal which 'was suffering from diarrhoea, had pus running from its nostrils, and an open wound in its side through which fluids were drawn off from time to time.'[12] He was not unaware of the cruelty involved but believed that his higher calling exempted him from such considerations: 'A physiologist is not a man of fashion, he is a man of science, absorbed by the scientific idea which he pursues: he no longer hears the cry of animals, he no longer sees the blood that flows, he sees only his idea and perceives only organisms concealing problems which he intends to solve.'[13] Bernard is the prototype which scientific education seeks to emulate.

Naturally, those denied such an education have difficulty achieving this kind of detachment. Bernard's wife was a case in point. She endured his work for twenty-four years but finally left him. She is said to have set up a home for lost dogs, to save them from the vivisectionists. In fact, she and her daughters were rumoured to walk the streets of Paris in search of strays, to save them from their famous husband and father.[14]

But even within the profession there were physiologists who lacked Bernard's perfect detachment. Some adopted a routine precaution: at the outset of an experiment they would sever the vocal cords of the animal on the table, so that it could not bark or cry out during the operation.[15] This is a significant action, for in doing it the physiologist was simultaneously doing two other things: he was denying his humanity, and he was affirming it. He was denying it in that he was able to cut the vocal cords and then pretend that the animal could feel no pain, that it was merely the machine Descartes had claimed it to be. But he was also affirming his humanity in that, had he not cut the cords, the desperate cries of the animal would have told him what he already knew, that it *was* a sentient, feeling being and not a machine at all.

That act is an appropriate metaphor for the creation of a biological scientist out of an animal-lover. The rite of passage into the scientific way of being centres on the ability to apply the knife to the vocal cords, not just of the dog on the table, but of life itself. Inwardly, he must be able to sever the cords in his own consciousness. Outwardly, the effect must be the destruction of the larynx of the biosphere, an action essential to the transformation of the world into a material object subservient to the laws of classical physics. In effect, he must deny life in order to study it. That paradox is at the root of the whole endeavour, and perhaps at the root of the environmentalists' dilemma. Consider this statement by one of the first effective proponents of modern science, Galileo:

Now I say that whenever I conceive any material or corporeal substance, I immediately feel the need to think of it as bounded, and as having this or that shape; as being large or small in relation to other things, and in some specific place at any given time; as being in motion or at rest; as touching or not touching some other body; and as being one in a number, or few, or many. From these conditions I cannot separate such a substance by any stretch of my imagination. But that it must be white or red, bitter or sweet, noisy or silent, and of sweet or foul odor, my mind does not feel compelled to bring in as necessary accompaniments. Without the senses as our guides, reason or imagination unaided would probably never arrive at qualities like these. Hence I think that tastes, odors, colors, and so on are no more than mere names so far as the object in which we place them is concerned, and that they reside only in the consciousness. Hence if the living creatures were removed, all these qualities would be wiped away and annihilated. But since we have imposed upon them special names, distinct from those of the other and real qualities mentioned pre-

viously, we wish to believe that they really exist as actually different from those.[16]

Notice the condition upon which Galileo's new science depends: 'if the living creatures were removed.' As Marjorie Grene points out, this great 'book of nature' from which Galileo claims to read describes a nature *deprived of life*. The condition for discovering the *real* properties of nature – number, size, shape, and so forth – is the exclusion of life and all the qualities dependent on it. It is more than a little strange to think of people accepting as normal a view of nature from which they are excluded. Galileo asks us to see the world as it would be if we did not exist. And what we now regard as nature is this objectified nature, in contrast with the world of our immediate experience. 'Thus,' concludes the biological theorist Ludwig von Bertalanffy, 'what is specific of our human experience, is progressively eliminated. What eventually remains is only a system of mathematical relations.'[17]

The Limits of Ecology

All of us, by virtue of our membership in a science-dominated culture, have adopted the abstraction of Galileo as our definition of nature. And in denying our immediate experience in deference to that abstraction we have gone some way towards cutting the earthly vocal cords ourselves. This is not an esoteric phenomenon confined to the laboratory. How many of us have, as the psychiarist J.H. van den Berg suggests, replied to our children's questions about the nature of the world and of life in terms that only make sense in a Galilean context? When the child asks: 'why have the leaves turned red?' or 'why does it snow?' we launch into explanations which have no obvious connection with the question. Leaves are red because it is cold, we say. What has cold to do with colour? How is the child to know that we are talking of abstract connections between atmospheric conditions and leaf chemistry? And why should he care? The child has asked 'why,' not 'how,' and certainly not 'how much.' And why should he care that the molecular structure of water is believed to be such that at low temperatures it forms rigid bonds which make it appear as ice or snow? None of these abstractions says anything about what the child experiences: the redness of leaves

and the cool, tickling envelopment by snow. The living response would
be quite different.

'Why are the leaves red, Dad?' 'Because it is so beautiful, child. Don't you see
how beautiful it is, all these autumn colors?'
 There is no truer answer. That is how the leaves are red. An answer which does
not invoke questions, which does not lead the child into an endless series of
questions, to which each answer is a threshold. The child will hear later on that a
chemical reaction occurs in those leaves. It is bad enough, then; let us not make
the world uninhabitable for the child too soon.[18]

One may wonder what van den Berg has against 'objective' descriptions, or indeed what this issue of a scientific mode of thought has to do
with our central concern, the environmental movement. But van den
Berg strikes a familiar and important note at the end of this quotation:
'let us not make the world uninhabitable for the child too soon.' It may
be fair to suggest that the issue of habitation is central to the environmental movement. The environmentalist is concerned with the *quality*
of life, a term often misinterpreted as the *quantity* of life, a measure
of material consumption. And that quality is discerned with the faculties
of the human being, the very ones excluded by Galileo as irrelevant to
a proper understanding of the world. What van den Berg protests is the
exclusion of what is most important to living beings.
 Consider two things: the motivation of the environmentalist and the
nature of the ally to whom he has turned for help. During much of
the history of the environmental movement it has been apparent that the
incentive to preservation was personal and emotional. It was a reflection of the value experienced by certain persons in the face of nature.
But the arrival of ecology and of all forms of resource management
has made it possible to be that contradictory being, a dispassionate environmentalist. That is, it is now possible to regard the world as a com-
posite of neutral material, and at the same time to frame suggestions for
action based upon a mechanistic understanding of natural processes.
As noted, this has made the environmental arguments much more pre-
sentable to government agencies and to a disinterested public, but it
does so at the expense of that central feature of the environmental
movement: passionate involvement. This is not to suggest that environ-

mental advocates have become indifferent to their subject, but the underlying assumptions have shifted significantly. In order to make use of his new ally the environmentalist has had virtually to forsake his *raison d'être*. In learning to use numbers to talk about the world he forgets that his initial revolt was partly precipitated by people using numbers to talk about the world. The ecologist as a scientist is not genuinely able to help the environmentalist because he cannot admit the importance of many of their claims (although, of course, as individuals many ecologists do so, in a somewhat schizoid way). The ecologist is forced to treat nature as essentially non-living, as a machine to be dissected, interpreted, and manipulated. As the ecologist Robert Peters puts it in a recent paper: 'ecology disappoints because it treats this material scientifically; and science is usually appreciated only after a long and rigorous education.'[19]

This is a difficult pill for both ecologists and environmentalists to swallow. After all, most ecologists share the values of the nature-lover, at least initially. And for environmentalists it is difficult to imagine how anyone can spend his or her life studying nature without experiencing a great personal involvement and an emotional commitment. Indeed, since ecology seems to have supplanted natural history as the 'official' form of nature-study, it is often seen as a continuation of that older enterprise. But as Peters has argued, the two are quite dissimilar. He suggests that the remaining vestiges of natural history must be excised if ecology is to attain the status of a proper science. Natural history is appreciative and personal, while 'the goal of biology, ecology, or any science is prediction.' Even such activities as species identification, so dear to the naturalist, may be serious impediments for the scientific ecologist, who might be better advised to concentrate on the mass of chlorophyll in a pond ecosystem or on phosphorous utilization.

If natural history promotes an understanding of the world, it is in the same sense that we understand another person. We recognize this or that behaviour as typical of a particular individual and, perhaps, we feel that, in his place, we might behave or think in the same way. But we do not necessarily control or predict what he will do. To a scientist understanding implies prediction, whereas the understanding of a naturalist is an empathy with nature or some part of nature.[20]

Peters is correct: the two are fundamentally different. And part of the confusion about ecology arises from the assumption that natural history *is* ecology. But as a science ecology is concerned, not with experiencing or appreciating nature, but with predicting and controlling the living material of the world. This mis-fit between the nature-lover and the ecologist should not surprise us, for it was inevitable. And Peters is not the first to try to drive an official wedge between natural history and ecology. A.G. Tansley is famous as the originator of the term 'ecosystem.' But he was also an opponent of certain other ecologists who harboured what he considered fuzzy-minded or mystical theories about nature. He rejected any suggestion of intent in nature, such as the notion that communities of organisms develop on pre-arranged lines towards a specific 'climax' association. In contrast, as Worster points out in his excellent history of ecology, 'Tansley hoped to purge from ecology all that was not subject to quantification and analysis, all those obscurities that had been a part of its baggage at least since the Romantic period. He would rescue it from the status of a vaguely mysterious, moralizing "point of view" and make of it instead a hard-edged, mechanistic, nothing-but discipline, marching in closed ranks with the other sciences.'[21] For his purposes Tansley's concept of the ecosystem was an inspired one, for it allowed him to direct attention to exchanges of energy and chemical elements. He felt that ecology had stagnated because of its inability to reduce nature to the laws of physico-chemical activity. The discovery of the ecosystem concept ended this. 'It marked ecology's coming of age as an adjunct of physical science. Henceforth it would gradually cease to be set off as a kind of comprehensive biology, and would instead be increasingly absorbed into the physics of energy systems.'[22]

This is precisely what has happened – ecology has become a branch of classical physics, in spirit if not in exact content. The results of ecological research are therefore predetermined in some measure. Starting with mechanistic assumptions, it can only discover machines. Consequently it will always seem reasonable to assume that we can manipulate the ecomachine. If we can fix engines, we can fix ecosystems. And breaking one need not be any more serious than breaking the other, as long as we do not lose the pieces. Peters concludes that 'natural history can convince us that the earth is worth salvation but it is too intricate, too personal, and too impractical to provide us with the tools necessary to save it. This is the work of science.'[23] Science can provide means but not ends. Worster concludes that 'the best that might be hoped for from the science of ecology, at present, is the more careful management of those resources, to preserve the biotic capital while maximizing the income.'[24] In other words, ecology can help us pursue the goals we have already set for ourselves: the maximum utilization of the earth as raw material in the support of one species. Yet environmentalism has typically been a revolt against the presumption that this is indeed a suitable goal. True, a pursuit of efficient exploitation may entail various conservation measures, and even some preservation if it is deemed in man's self-interest. But it does not address the question of ends – why are we doing all this in the first place?   ✳✳ Exactly!

Resourcism and Reification

Ecology can help one to criticize inefficient exploitation or destructive utilization of nature, but it cannot help illuminate the experience that inspires one to be an environmentalist. But, of course, it promised no more, and delivered just what should have been expected. Compare Roszak's description of ecology, cited on page 5 above, with Peters's contention that ecology's goal is prediction and control: 'Predictive power is the touchstone of science, the ultimate criterion against which every scientific hypothesis can be tested.'[25] Can this be the science which Roszak claims is 'wholistic, receptive, trustful, largely non-tampering, deeply grounded in aesthetic intuition'? With such expectations ecology is bound to disappoint. It can help us manage natural resources, but it does not challenge the concept of 'resourcism.' Ecology can help us argue that a bog should be preserved because it serves us by detoxifying wastes. But the act of justifying the bog as a glorified septic tank entails acceptance of the very scale of evaluation which is the environmentalist's most formidable adversary. Worster notes that 'in reducing the living world to ingredients that could be easily measured and graphed, the ecologist was also in danger of removing all the residual emotional impediments to unrestrained manipulation. To describe nature as an organism or community suggested one kind of environmental behavior by man; to speak of it as but "a momentary stay against

entrophy" suggested a wholly different behavior, and as good as removed it from the ethical realm altogether.'[26]

Resourcism is a kind of modern religion which casts all of creation
into categories of utility. By treating everything as homogeneous matter
in search of a use it devalues all. Yet its most dangerous aspect is its
apparent good intention. By describing something as a resource we seem
to have cause to protect it. But all we really have is a licence to exploit
it. 'Violence,' says R.D. Laing, 'cannot be seen through the sights of
positivism.'

*A woman grinds stuff down a goose's neck through a funnel. Is this a
description of cruelty to an animal? She disclaims any motivation or intention of
cruelty. If we were to describe this scene 'objectively' we would only be denuding
it of what is 'objectively' or, better, ontologically present in the situation. Every
description presupposes our ontological premises as to the nature (being) of
man, of animals, and of the relationship between them.*

*If an animal is debased to a manufactured piece of produce, a sort of
biochemical complex — so that its flesh and organs are simply material that has a
certain texture in the mouth (soft, tender, tough), a taste, perhaps a smell —
then to describe the animal* positively *in those terms is to debase oneself by debasing being itself.*[27]

To describe a tree as an oxygen-producing device or a bog as a
filtering agent is equally violent, equally debasing to being itself. For an
environmentalist to so argue is to betray his cause utterly. It is as if,
striving for position A in preference to position B, he pauses half way
and redefines B as A, so that he can stay where he was and still claim
victory. Absolutely nothing has been achieved in the struggle of the
environmental movement, over the long run. In combatting exploitation, environmentalists have tutored the developer in the art of careful
exploitation. In combatting the devaluation of nature they have embraced a method of study which takes such devaluation as its starting-
point. And in claiming victory through the spread of resourcism they
have rejected their own moral position and given support to a cultural
imperative that neutralizes and debases life itself.

This may seem an unjust condemnation of the many people who call
themselves environmentalists and who have worked tirelessly to de-

fend their world in the best way they could. But, of course, we are not questioning intentions or sincerity, only the consequences of this kind of action. Once adopted, resourcism transforms all relationships to nature into a simple subject-object or user-used one. Even something as apparently idiosyncratic as landscape beauty is now being transformed into a resource and described quantitatively. By asking a series of observers which scenes are most desirable researchers have obtained a definition of excellence (or at least of 'most preferred') in nature. And by searching out physical correlates to these preferences they have been able to predict which locations will be judged aesthetically superior. Consequently, the aesthetic merit or 'visual resource potential' of every site can be taken into account when making planning decisions. Aside from the fact that this amounts to creating a simple rating system for landscape, like the Nielson ratings for television, it also promotes the idea of beauty as simply another resource, like timber or mineral content; it is another material thing that can be utilized by humans. But it is especially obvious in this instance that what we are accomplishing is the reification of an abstraction,[28] turning beauty into an object. We know from historical records that tastes in landscape are notoriously variable – we see in nature what we are prepared to look for. And we travel not so much to visit nature as to see the outward expression of our own abstractions. Given the right components, we can search out a proper landscape, one that reflects the standards of the artists of the picturesque whose work we all grew up with.[29] And since we accept only the physical world as real, we ask only which sites are beautiful, never 'in what way is each site beautiful?' In deciding to find a resource we have to transform landscape beauty into something quite different from what it was before. Rather than an experience or a way of perceiving the world, aesthetics becomes a collector's search for special things. As things, landscapes can be measured and managed, created and destroyed, traded off against other objects and uses. Resourcism, in reducing all values to one, may well be the Trojan horse of the industrial state.

To return briefly to our earlier analogy: the attitude of resourcism applied to the black man on trial would force us to transform him as well. We could not think of him as a human being, possessed of intrinsic worth or innate rights. Instead he would have to be thought of as a neutral object with utility to society. And we could measure him, judge his worth, and decide that, whatever his drawbacks and misdemeanours, he has such-and-such amount of social utility and should therefore be preserved for future use. He is a 'human resource,' as the bureaucrats unashamedly put it. In other words, he would have to be treated as an object, a commodity – a slave. Resourcism requires that we think of the world as the slavers thought of their human merchandise. Indeed, the domination of nature and the domination of man go hand in hand, as William Leiss has shown: they reflect the same assumptions of reality.[30]

Notice what has happened in this example. We have 'saved' the man – or at least his body and genes – by turning him into a useful object, a resource. But we have lost precisely what we set out to defend – his right to an independent existence and recognition of his intrinsic worth. To save him, we enslave him, and so paradoxically aid in his destruction. Is this progress by any standard – 'saving' something that looks like a man, or something that looks like a wolf, or a piece of real estate that looks like a nineteenth-century landscape painting? This is certainly not what the environmentalist, or the civil-rights worker, sets out to accomplish. But one may come to accept the saving of an appearance in order to achieve the appearance of victory. Nothing really changes at all – a case of what Hemingway reputedly called 'mistaking motion for action.'

The Map Is Not the Territory

Naturally, the problem of trying to express something that is not formally recognized in the lexicon of society is not unique to the environmentalist, or to our times. It is probably inevitable that any social paradigm must concentrate on some aspects of reality and play down others. This may pose no serious problem as long as the social reality is reasonably consistent with the experience of the individual. But when a gap appears between what one experiences as real and what is officially recognized as real, conflict is inevitable. What I have suggested above is that the environmentalist's experience does not fit with the official view of the world, which derives in part from Galileo's new book of nature, devoid of life but resplendent with things for use. The challenge has been perceived as one of translating the environmentalist's experience into terms that can be recognized officially. But as we have seen, that ultimately entails a renunciation of the very values that the environmentalist set out to defend. In the long run, the environmentalist must either capitulate or question his own sanity. Unless, of course, he becomes aware that his shortcomings may not be his at all.

E.F. Schumacher has discussed this possibility in his *A Guide for the Perplexed*. He relates his discovery that his own confusion was not an inner failing:

All through school and university I had been given maps of life and knowledge on which there was hardly a trace of many of the things that I most cared about and that seemed to me to be of the greatest possible importance to the conduct of my life. I remembered that for many years my perplexity had been complete; and no interpreter had come along to help me. It remained complete until I ceased to suspect the sanity of my perceptions and began, instead, to suspect the soundness of the maps.[31]

Clearly, the values detected by the environmentalist in the natural world are among the features missing from the official maps of reality. In searching out the source of this bias Schumacher concludes that 'the maps produced by modern materialistic Scientism leave all the questions that really matter unanswered; more than that, they deny the validity of the questions.'[32] Schumacher is not speaking specifically of environmental questions, but his comments are entirely appropriate to the subject at hand. And it is this kind of realization that has precipitated an internal re-assessment of the environmental movement in recent years. Certainly the majority go on as before, fighting with whatever means are at their disposal. But a significant number are questioning the long-term efficacy of this tactic, and have begun to call instead for the development of maps which adequately represent the features they consider most significant. They accept the futility of trying to defend that which is not even admitted to exist, along with the realization that, until new maps are provided, there is very little prospect of achieving environmental protection.

This is not to suggest that the environmental movement has been split into two rival factions, one practical and reasonable, the other uncompromising and introspective. Indeed, the movement has long been too fragmented to permit easy characterization. But it may be fair to say that there is a polarity of opinion within the various sectors of the movement. Once it became apparent that there was some divergence, various writers undertook to describe and explain it, and inevitably new terminology emerged to permit a comparison of these poles of the environmental movement. The first to do so successfully was Arne Naess, a Norwegian philosopher. It might be more accurate to describe his classification as a recognition of a central core in the movement and a periphery of application, rather than as a strict duality. The distinction he made was between the 'shallow' and the 'deep, long-range' ecology movements.[33] In a more recent discussion Bill Devall has spoken of 'reformist environmentalism' in contrast to 'deep ecology,' and he has noted other terminology that has arisen to describe this new turn in environmentalism, such as 'eco-philosophy' or 'foundational ecology' or 'the new natural philosophy.'

There are two great streams of environmentalism in the latter half of the twentieth century. One stream is reformist, attempting to control some of the worst of the air and water pollution and inefficient land use practices in industrialized nations and to save a few of the remaining pieces of wildlands as 'designated wilderness areas.' The other stream supports many of the reformist goals but is revolutionary, seeking a new metaphysics, epistemology, cosmology, and environmental ethics of person/planet.[34]

Although Devall does not suggest that deep ecology is revolutionary in the political sense, he does claim that it 'questions the fundamental premises of the dominant social paradigm.' In contrast, reformist environmentalism tries to improve living standards without challenging any underlying beliefs. We have been discussing the consequences of that strategy up to this point. Writers such as Devall and Naess help to crystallize the distinction between the environmentalist who tries to understand and to act in accordance with his own conscience and experience of value and those who settle for trying to improve the means of managing and exploiting the planet. Until now I have been suggesting that many in the environmental movement have a sense that all is not well, that there is a mis-fit between environmental values and main-

stream societal attitudes. Devall describes the reflections of a significant subgroup within the environmental movement which has recognized the source of the dilemma and has set out to explain the problem
and initiate a revision. Deep ecology sets itself the task of confronting the
'dominant social paradigm' that stands in the way of any significant
change in man-enviroment relations. Naess speaks of the need 'to
integrate in the world the value priorities themselves,' and warns against
'the cleavage of value from facts' that derives primarily from 'an over-
estimation of certain scientific traditions from Galileo, confusing the
instrumental excellence of the mechanistic world view with its properties as a whole philosophy.'[35] Clearly this constitutes a challenge to that
tradition which insists on the severing of earthly vocal cords and which
requires that we live in a neutral world, governed by instrumental
relationships and expediency.

Accustomed as we are to thinking in terms of physical action, we
immediately ask: what does a deep ecologist actually do? According to
Devall:

> *There is no political party of 'deep ecology,' no cadre of political revolutionar-*
> *ies. This is not an appropriate approach for deep ecologists. No frontal confronta-*
> *tions with reformist environmentalists or with the dominant social/political*
> *order is desired. It would be counter-productive by making people more defensive*
> *of their ideological position. Deep ecology is not an attempt to add one more*
> ideology *in the crowded field of modern ideologies. Deep ecologists are questing*
> *for ways to liberate and cultivate the ecological consciousness.*[36]

Naess strikes a similar note, suggesting that what is required of the
individual is not engagement in overt action but simply standing up to be
counted. A plain testimonial will help precipitate the desired change.
'What we ask is *not* that they should fight for the change to the better,
but just that they should tell about it in public, make it crystal clear. A
small minority will then fight – with joy – supported by that considerable section.'[37]

This is still not an answer that will satisfy everyone; it still sounds
uncomfortably passive to the western ear, almost like primitive Christi-
anity in its tactics. In fact, judging from what Naess's 'small minority' has
accomplished in Norway, it may not be as passive as it seems.[38] But,

even so, the significant point is its requirement that the individual declare his belief, with no attempt to camouflage it with alleged uses or
benefit-cost estimates. It requires the individual to bear witness to his
own personal experience of the world, even though that be in conflict
with social reality, and even though it risks ridicule from the majority.

Romanticism: An Analogy

The problem of having to express something that has a dubious standing in society is certainly not unique to the environmentalist. Neither
is the suggestion that it be attempted by bearing witness to one's personal
experience. One of the most notable movements to attempt this is one
with which the environmental movement is frequently compared – dis-
paragingly. For, like it or not, there are parallels with the Romantic
movement of the later eighteenth and nineteenth centuries. Consider,
for example, Devall's description of a major theme of deep ecology:

*In deep ecology, the wholeness and integrity of person/planet together with the
principle of what Arne Naess calls 'biological equalitarianism' are the most important ideas. Man is an integral part of nature, not over or apart from nature.
Man is a 'plain citizen' of the biosphere, not its conqueror or manager.*[39]

In the Romantic tradition the ideas of wholeness and of man as a part of
nature are of similar importance. According to Worster, 'at the very
core of this Romantic view of nature was what later generations would
come to call an ecological perspective: that is, a search for holistic or
integrated perception, an emphasis on interdependence and relatedness
in nature, and an intense desire to restore man to a place of intimate
intercourse with the vast organism that constitutes the earth.[40]
    At this level the similarity is apparent. But unfortunately Romanti-
cism also had its 'shallow' and 'deep' streams, and, as with environmentalism, the shallow one is used to characterize the movement. Hence
'Romantic' has come to be used as a synonym for 'sentimental' or
'utopian.' It has also been used to describe persons who desire a return
to some idealized state of nature – a characterization frequently used
against environmentalists as well. Unlike the environmentalist, however,
the Romantic cannot speak to condemn this error, except through the

careful scholarship of writers such as M.H. Abrams. He has noted that it is 'an extreme historical injustice that Romanticism has been identified with the cult of the noble savage and the cultural idea of a return to an early stage of simple and easeful "nature".'[41] On the contrary, he says, men such as Schiller rejected this idea, claiming that 'the "nature which you envy in the nonrational is unworthy of your respect and longing"' and that 'our only possible road is not "back to Arcadia" but "onward to Elysium".'[42] It may be, then, that much of the reason for resisting the comparison between the environmental and the Romantic movements stems from a misunderstanding of what the Romantic movement was. Without discounting the many excesses of that movement, we must admit that the popular image of the Romantics is largely unjustified and their central tenets largely forgotten.[43]

Challenges to conventional wisdom can most easily be dismissed by regarding them as nonsensical or impractical. It is hardly surprising to find these charges raised against both movements. But in the case of the Romantics at least, the dismissal may stem in part from the opacity of their central message. For they challenged not only conventional beliefs but the very process of formulating beliefs.

In describing Romanticism – no mean task, given the range of definitions available, many of them contradictory – Robert Combs has concluded that 'Romanticism is not a description of certain men at all, but a description of a way of behaving, as it is reflected in particular documents that have survived since the nineteenth century.'[44] Romanticism is not so much a set of themes or beliefs as an overall approach to life. Furthermore, 'all these documents share a common focus on the discrepancy between the formulation of the sense of value and the experience of it.'[45] This is essentially what I have been describing in the case of the environmentalist, whose experience finds no analogue in the intellectual maps of society. And when it becomes impossible to reconcile one's personal experience of the world with the official account, one's resulting behaviour is certain to appear abnormal or even revolutionary.

The dissonance that stirred the Romantics to action was engendered by the scientific assumptions that were taking hold in the eighteenth century. The abstractions developed through classical physics found increasing application in all areas of society, and, as we have

already noted, they soon came to be taken as the revealed truth
instead of as inspired assumptions. The Romantic's problem was that
he still saw them as assumptions, and was moved to describe the
emperor's new clothes to all and sundry. The Romantic was seldom the
anti-science or anti-reason fanatic he is accused of being. He could comprehend the usefulness of the physicist's assumptions within the strictly defined boundaries of the science. But he could not accept its projection beyond that realm. He made it his business to understand how a
society comes to adopt a particular view of reality, and, as that process
became apparent to him, he felt compelled to try to demonstrate the
perils of constructing a needlessly restrictive world-view. 'Unquestioned
beliefs,' says Combs, 'are the real authorities of a culture. Therefore,
if an individual can express what is undeniably real to him *without*
invoking any authority beyond his own experience, he is transcending
the belief systems of his culture.'[46] This the Romantic did, trying to
express that personal experience without translating it into the abstractions of the dominant social paradigm. And he started with the
experience of nature. According to Alfred North Whitehead, 'we are
here witnessing a conscious reaction against the whole tone of the
eighteenth century. That century approached nature with the abstract
analysis of science, whereas Woodsworth opposes to the scientific
abstractions his full concrete experience.'[47] But in turning to personal
experience one forgoes the security of an established belief system
with which to make sense of the world and exposes oneself to whatever
comes. It means becoming a perpetual outsider. The gain for the
individual is the experience itself and the continual surprise of existence.
But for the rest of us it is the exposure of our own beliefs. In describing what simply *is*, the Romantic simultaneously reveals by contrast what
we *suppose* to be. The Romantic is a constant beginner in life, always
learning, never content to be instructed by others. He 'embraces the
perversity of truth instead of the complicity of agreement.'[48]

The environmentalist need not be defensive when he is compared
with the Romantics of the past, although he may find it necessary to
spell out which traits he shares with them. If the comparison is meant to
imply nostalgia for a utopian past, then it is unfair to both groups. But
if it refers to a rejection of fragmentation and an emphasis on personal
experience, it may be reasonably accurate, and it may help to clarify

the position of the environmentalist. It is important to note, however, that the Romantic did not restrict his interests to nature alone; in fact some, like William Blake, paid very little attention to nature. But while others such as Wordsworth obviously did have a very deep involvement with nature, it is probably fair to say that for most the choice of nature as a central theme was largely pragmatic. When you wish to pursue experience unsullied by social convention, it makes sense to look where those conventions are least plentiful. All of the world is 'translated' for us, in some degree, by the explanatory structure which is our social reality. Within society it is difficult to transcend that structure – it is all around us, constantly reinforced by the speech and behaviour of others. But wilderness is almost definable as the *absence* of social structure; it is the realm of reality that humans have *not* fully interpreted. It is the unknown, and as such it constituted the best choice for the Romantic experiment. The Romantics were not so much nature poets as reality-experimenters working in the environment least hostile to their project.

Related to this, and of particular relevance to the environmental movement, is the significance the Romantics attached to the relationship between man and nature. Convinced as they were that our cultural apparatus greatly coloured what we could perceive in the world, they were concerned with our decreasing facility for actually encountering nature. The Romantics maintained that the view of reality perpetrated by Locke and Newton deprived us of the most important aspects of the world and therefore transformed mankind as well. In choosing to regard only a limited range of experience as 'real,' the materialist alters what he sees and what he is. Hence the Romantic claim that 'man has lapsed into a fixed and "narrowed" mode of "single vision" by means of the physical eye alone, which sees reality as a multitude of isolated individuals in a dehumanized world,'[49] a sentiment we shall have cause to examine later. The rise in science, Blake argued, coincides with a drastic diminuition in human perception and, contrary to common belief, in human understanding as well.

But if the important facts of nature can be said to elude us when we attend to quantity and to visible surfaces, it is reasonable to ask what it was that Wordsworth found in nature that science could not. In answer, Whitehead reminds us that *it is emphatically not the case that Wordsworth hands over inorganic matter to the mercy of science, and concentrates on the faith that in the living organism there is some element that science cannot analyse. Of course he recognizes, what no one doubts, that in some sense living things are different from lifeless things. But that is not his main point. It is the brooding presence of the hills which haunts him. His main theme is nature in* solido, *that is to say, he dwells on that mysterious presence of surrounding things, which imposes itself on any separate element that we set up as an individual for its own sake. He always grasps the whole of nature as involved in the tonality of the particular instance.*[50]

At this point the relevance of Wordsworth and his fellows may begin to escape us. Their descriptions may impress us, even move us. But to speak of 'the brooding presence of the hills' or of 'that mysterious presence of the surrounding things' as if they are real is certain to strain our credulity. These are subjective, are they not? The projections of a poetic mind? But Whitehead's point is that we do experience such things, whether or not we attribute any significance to them. And since we do experience them, just as we experience the size or shape of the items in a landscape, is it not curious that we judge one experience to be real, the other a fabrication? Wordsworth, says Whitehead, 'expresses the concrete facts of our apprehension, facts which are distorted in the scientific analysis.'[51] Like Wordsworth, we all bring the weight of our own experience to bear against the model of the world proposed by science. But unlike him, we fail to recognize the paradox of choosing to believe the abstraction in preference to the experience. To use Schumacher's analogy again, we would prefer to use a societal map, even though it leaves out the places most important to us, rather than to rely on our own sense of direction.

The action that is being asked of environmentalists today is to recognize this paradox and publicly to decline to use the old map. Instead of accepting beliefs that trivialize the experience of living and assert the reality of a valueless world, the environmentalist is urged to attest to his own experience of a meaningful, valuable, colourful world. Environmentalism, like Romanticism before it, is essentially 'a protest on behalf of value.'

Remembering the poetic rendering of our concrete experience, we see at once that the element of value, of being valuable, of having value, of being an end in itself, of being something which is for its own sake, must not be omitted in any account of an event as the most concrete actual something. 'Value' is the word I use for the intrinsic reality of an event. Value is an element which permeates through and through the poetic view of nature.[52]

The environmentalist must demonstrate his experience of value as a feature of reality and reject any maps that are deficient in this feature. At the outset I suggested a very broad definition of an environmentalist as one who bears a concern for a world in which he experiences a sense of value. Whitehead brings us back to this starting-point and leaves us to contemplate how this protest on behalf of value is to proceed.

CHAPTER TWO

The Fields of Self

The Search for Boundaries

The public expectations of the environmental movement have fallen out of register with the aspirations of thoughtful figures within that movement. While it was once fairly safe to assume that the goals of the movement were simply the encouragement of responsible resource exploitation and the discouragement of actions which jeopardize the life-sustaining functions of the earth, these may no longer be adequate. With the realization that such goals are themselves determined by the assumptions of the industrial state, the role of the environmentalist is transformed. It is no longer possible to deal with environmental issues in isolation from the attitudes and assumptions that precipitated them in the first place. And if, as E.F. Schumacher suggests, there are massive defects in the societal maps upon which we rely for guidance, then clearly the first step in redirecting the environmental movement must entail a re-examination and eventual redrafting of those maps. Following that, other paths of action may become apparent – if indeed the issues still remain when the map is redrawn.

It is important to bear in mind that the concern expressed by environmentalists reflects an underlying assessment of the relation of man to nature. How we act towards the non-human is a consequence of our beliefs about how we should act and about what we are acting on. Indeed, Paul Shepard may have been entirely accurate in his suggestion that the central problem of human ecology is the relationship of mind to nature.[1] We must pay some attention to this problem before proceeding. The remarks that follow may sometimes seen tangential to our central concern, but they are intended to help us draw back for an overview. They may help to reveal the context in which environmentalism arises.

In raising doubts about the wisdom of relying on the biological sciences for support I was not attempting to disparage this discipline or to suggest that it has nothing to offer. Neither were my comments about the Romantics intended to suggest uncritical acceptance of that movement. Chapter 1 is simply an attempt to set aside our usual assumptions about how we must approach environmentalism. Uncritical acceptance of ecology can be just as damaging as uncritical acceptance of Romanticism, and, perhaps, uncritical rejection of either. At the very least the Romantic movement serves as a warning of the fate of ideas which become distorted and trivialized as they become more popular and more understandable. Books such as M.H. Abrams's *Natural Supernaturalism* serve as welcome correctives to our stereotyped opinion of the Romantic movement, and the parallels with the environmental movement can be observed in such works as Theodore Roszak's *Where the Wasteland Ends*. But, for the moment, the most interesting parallel between the Romantics and the environmentalists is their shared dilemma in encountering societal maps which exclude that which is most important, and their response to that realization. So far the environmentalists have sought to adapt themselves to the existing map; the Romantics apparently regarded this response as futile.

Perhaps a useful analogy for the social construction of reality[2] is the production of a landscape photograph. If we assume that there is a *normal* photograph that represents what is actually present in the world, then the act accomplished by society is the taking of one small portion of that image and pretending it is the whole. That is, we enlarge this selected portion to fill the entire frame, and then pretend that is all there ever was in the scene. The doctored photograph is then hung in every mind, like the mandatory images of aging dictators on the walls of government offices. But when one finds important details missing, it is natural to feel uncomfortable, or even to protest the hanging of this scene. Often the offended party will offer his own view, equally limited, and demand that it be substituted for the official one. But the Romantics protested not just the selection of one portion over another but the act of selection itself; they demanded that the entire scene be left intact. And the entire scene was all that was experienced, not just that which fit comfortably with one theory or another. In effect, the Romantics required that each individual rephotograph the world for himself, without special lenses or subsequent manipulation. This they saw as the only way of avoiding the distortion which inevitably comes with any act of selection.

The lesson the Romantics offer is one that at the outset environmentalists, or at least their precursors, knew full well. It is simply that one must be true to one's own experience of value in the world, must embrace 'the perversity of truth instead of the complicity of agreement.' This may explain why the most effective figures in the movement have been amateurs whose dedication was not diluted by professional or vested interests.[3] But it is advice more easily given than acted upon. As a member of industrial society it is difficult for any enviromentalist to step fully outside that society's assumptions, or to make sense of it if he does. Still, this is a challenge that cannot be entirely ignored. As a first step we must ask how our experience of the world compares with our beliefs about it. In doing so we will have to rely on insight drawn from writers in diverse fields of study. Oddly enough, it may be easiest to begin with the field discussed earlier, biology. For even if orthodox biological assumptions are inadequate to sustain the environmental movement, the observations of individual biologists may be especially helpful.

The writer John Fowles has argued that much of western art 'betrays our love of clearly defined boundaries, unique identities, of the individual thing released from the confusion of the background.' But this is true not only of art. Throughout our culture clear distinctions are sought after. Structuralists regard this as a normal attribute of the human mind, with its need to form categories out of continua. But according to Fowles, 'even the simplest knowledge of the names and habits of flowers or trees starts this distinguishing and individuating process, and removes us a step from total reality toward anthropocentrism; that is, it acts mentally as an equivalent of the camera's viewfinder.'[4] But this says nothing about the reality of the boundaries we discover; it simply says that we like to find them. Perhaps, given our strong reliance on vision, this should not surprise us. But if we are to ask what aspects of reality are diminished through this prejudice, we must temporarily suspend our belief in a world of separate things. What do we find in the world when we stop attending to sharp boundaries? Do we actually experience ourselves as just one thing among many? Does any creature?

To begin with evidence of the kind we can most easily accept, biology offers us some insight into the question of separate existences. Of course, ecology itself is a denial of this in some measure, since it asserts that there are links between everything. But this does not challenge the notion of separate, skin-encapsulated beings. As we have noted earlier, there is nothing particularly subversive about ecology as normally applied. But its most basic premise, that of interrelatedness, could be subversive, if taken literally. That is, if we go beyond regarding interrelated as meaning 'causally connected' and consider it as indicating an actual intermingling of various individuals, we find our assumptions of sharp boundaries challenged.

Organisms that defy classification have always been mildly troublesome for taxonomists. It can happen that what appear to be distinct species are simply different forms of the same one, or that a single specimen turns out to be a close collaboration between two disparate organisms. Evolution itself implies a plasticity of being which can be disconcerting to orderly minds, and it may be that some of the early opposition to Darwin came from those who could not relinquish their concept of a perfectly labelled and invariate universe. But perhaps the creatures that most blatantly challenge our belief in firm boundaries are those known as symbionts. What are we to make of lichen, composed of two unrelated organisms? The algal component provides photosynthetic ability, the fungal component structure and nutrient intake. The two are mutually dependent. Is the lichen a plant? A co-operative? What about colonial organisms, in which different individuals perform unique functions so that the community as a whole persists? Is the Portuguese man-of-war an animal or a colony of animals? Where does one draw the line?

Recently such questions have become even more difficult to resolve. Until now it has at least seemed safe to assume that whatever is in a cell is of that cell. Now it appears that the chloroplasts within the plant cell, which permit the plant to utilize solar energy, behave independently of the cell. They may have originated as separate organisms and become so closely associated as to appear indistinguishable from the rest of the plant.[5] In that case what we take to be a single organism may actually be more like the lichen, an instance of mutualism in which the fates of two beings are so intertwined as to make them almost indistinguishable. Is a plant a plant, or a co-operative system of formerly independent creatures?

But still more disruptive of our search for absolute boundaries is the recent suggestion that even humans share in this kind of ambiguity. We have long known that we exist in close alliance with some other species, such as the intestinal bacteria that assist our digestive efforts. But it now appears that some of the organelles in our cells are quite as independent as the chloroplasts in plants. Mitochondria, the energy-providing structures within each cell, replicate independently of the cell and are composed of RNA which is dissimilar to that of the rest of the cell. Apparently the mitochondria move into the cells like colonists and continue their separate existence within. We cannot exist without them, and yet they may not strictly be 'us.' Does this mean that we must regard ourselves as colonies? Or is this merely a semantic quibble? After all, what difference does it make that the parts are not what they seemed, so long as they act as a distinct organism? But is it strictly distinct, complete unto itself? In a fascinating review of bacteriological research D. Reanny has outlined the difficulties that arise with the realization that mammalian evolution could probably not have occurred as rapidly as it did by mutation and selection alone.[6] There must have been some kind of acceleration, perhaps by allowing different expression of the genes present without resorting to gross alteration of the genetic material. That is, the genetic keyboard could remain about the same while different selections are performed on it. Such a phenomenon is known to occur in bacteria. There are 'extra-chromosomal elements' that can perform the role of cellular conductor, orchestrating new and resistant strains of bacterial cells to combat the extravagant barrage of antibiotics which flows through humans and their domesticated animals. Perhaps the most significant aspect of this phenomenon is that these are *extra*-chromosomal elements; that is, they are not part of what has been regarded as the control centre of the cell. They are

independent, and they are transferable. An extra-chromosomal element
can move from one cell to another, which means that a new evolutionary advance can be spread throughout the population very quickly,
without the lengthy process of mutation and selection. Creatures can
'infect' each other with evolutionary transformation. More shocking still,
these elements appear to be transmissible not only between individuals of the same species but between species as well. This means that it is
conceivable that groups of species, perhaps whole communities of
organisms, could, in a sense, co-evolve. They are all quite literally interrelated.

This is the potentially subversive realization that ecology can offer –
but only if it is taken literally rather than as an indicator of causal
connectedness. Where do we draw the line between one creature and
another? Where does one stop and the other begin? Is there even a
boundary between you and the non-living world, or will the atoms of
this page be part of *you* tomorrow? In short, how can you make any
sense of the concept of man as a discrete entity? How can the proper
study for man be man if it is impossible for man to exist out of context?
In light of this, the desire of some, particularly within the social
sciences and humanities, to deal exclusively with the fragment of reality
they term 'human' is nonsense.

What all this suggests is that our assumptions of separateness are
unacceptably simplistic, and that we might more closely approximate
the facts of existence by regarding ourselves less as objects than as sets
of relationships, or as processes in time rather than as static forms.
We must bear in mind that none of the evidence cited above is in
conflict with our accepted beliefs. But even within the framework of
normal science one cannot avoid the conclusion that emphasis on absolute distinctions between individuals can be misleading. Without resorting
to any kind of mysticism we still arrive at a realization of interrelatedness that challenges our Cartesian foundations. It is a short and
obvious step from here to think of organisms in terms of process. A tree,
we might say, is not so much a thing as a rhythm of exchange, or
perhaps a centre of organizational forces. Transpiration induces the
upward movement of water and dissolved materials, facilitating an
inflow from the soil. If we were aware of this rather than of the appearance of a tree-form, we might regard a tree as a centre of a force-field

towards which water is drawn. The object to which we attach significance is the configuration of the forces necessary to being a tree. The visible structure is the indicator that life is happening, just as a dog's bark is an indicator of the existence of that animal. The bark is not the dog any more than the visually delineated object is the tree. We do not mistake the bark for the dog, but we habitually mistake the shape for the tree. Only the visible is regarded as real. It is not necessarily the case that whatever exists must be sharply bounded; in fact, rigid attention to boundaries can obscure the act of being itself.

This description of a tree does not pose any conceptual challenge if we see it as if it were a supplementary note to our ordinary perceptions. It seems to be nothing more than an admission that there may be more going on in a plant than we can see – or, as we like to say, there are aspects of being a plant that science has not yet clarified, meaning that science has not yet put into visual terms. We might even be able to accept the notion of a plant as a force field, given our familiarity with such terminology in classical physics. But the implications of an interrelated world are much greater than this. It is not a case of a world yet to be visualized but of a world which defies simple vision. And that is much harder to accept, or even to see the need to accept. Yet when we examine our own personal understanding of the world, we may find that this concept is both necessary and familiar.

Organic Thought

On first reflection it would seem that the one thing of which we are certain is our own tangibility, our existence as physical presences. But when we explore the ways in which people actually do regard them-selves or intuit themselves, we find them less physical than we might expect. Certainly in the course of learning to stand, move, feel, hear, and so on we develop a body image. But this is not to say that we simply 'see' ourselves as creatures of a certain height with two arms and two legs. Rather, it is to say that we have an intangible image of a kind of force-field in which we feel ourselves to be present. In the course of an interview Jonathan Miller coined the phrase 'sculpting of the self' to describe this process of delineating a portion of the world as 'me.'[7] The image, once formed, can be highly resistant to change, or can shift quite abruptly. Even physical changes in the body may be denied by the image – that is, we tend to believe the image even more than visible evidence in some instances. In the phenomenon known as the 'phantom limb' patients who have had an amputation still sense the presence of the missing appendage. There remains a sensation of a field of existence designated 'self,' which is not necessarily concentric with the boundaries of the epidermis. Indeed, it may be normal for the field to extend outward and provide the personal space whose existence is all too evident when someone intrudes upon it.[8]

Furthermore, the self-image can apparently be altered without the body changing shape. Brain-damaged patients will sometimes disown an arm, for example.

Anosognosics who describe their arm as 'like a snake,' long and cold, do not, strictly speaking, fail to recognize its objective outline and, even when the patient looks unsuccessfully for his arm or fastens it in order not to lose it, he knows *well enough where his arm is, since that is where he looks for it and fastens it. If, however, patients experience their arm's space as something alien, if generally speaking I can feel my body's space as vast or minute despite the evidence of my senses, this is because there exists an affective presence and enlargement for which objective spatiality is not a sufficient condition, as anosognosia shows, and indeed not even a necessary condition, as is shown by the phantom arm.[9]*

Clearly, the fact that the arm appears to be attached to the body is of no consequence. If it is not part of the body image, it is not part of the self. This suggests that any attempt to treat people as purely physical manifestations is likely to end in misunderstanding. It is not what you see that delineates the person; it is what he senses to be himself. It may follow that assumptions about human needs based on purely physical criteria will also be found wanting. Maurice Merleau-Ponty claims that 'in order to describe the belief in the phantom limb and the unwillingness to accept mutilation, writers speak of a "driving into the unconscious" or "an organic repression". These un-Cartesian terms force us to form the idea of an organic thought through which the relation of the "psychic" to the "physiological" becomes conceivable.'[10] Certainly an 'organic thought' is not the phrase we would ordinarily choose to describe the individual human, but it may be a much more accurate rendering of the actual experience of being a self.

For our purposes it is the notion that the self is not necessarily defined by the body surface that is especially interesting. This means that there is some kind of involvement with the realm beyond the skin, and that the self is more a sense of self-potency throughout a region than a purely physical presence. 'My Being is not something that takes place inside my skin ... ; my Being, rather, is spread over a field or region which is the world of its care and concern.'[11] Such expressions as this one by William Barrett are initially puzzling to most of us, for while the words are familiar, the sense seems elusive. But this need not discourage us, if we remember that the task at hand is to question and possibly alter the societal maps that essentially define reality. If it is necessary to challenge such maps, it is inevitable that we wander through unfamiliar terrain. It would be more alarming if the alternatives we encountered seemed obvious, for this would no doubt indicate that the change in viewpoint was very minor. As it is, we have a suggestion that the individual may profitably be thought of not as a thing but as a field. In fact, Merleau-Ponty ends his classic *Phenomenology of Perception* with a quotation from Saint-Exupery: 'Man is but a network of relationships, and these alone matter to him.' The challenge before us is to see how such a shift in emphasis might alter our expectations of and behaviour towards the world at large.

It is perhaps Merleau-Ponty who has most thoroughly explored our misconceptions of man-in-world and elaborated the most detailed alternative. Central to his work is the notion of experience as a means of understanding. 'The world is not what I think, but what I live through,'[12] he says. It is a mistake to regard the individual as a separate body passively receiving sensory impressions of an external world. 'Our bodily experience of movement is not a particular case of knowledge; it provides us with a way of access to the world and the object, with a "praktognosia", which has to be recognized as original and perhaps as primary. My body has its world, or understands its world, without having to make use of my "symbolic" or "objectifying function".'[13] And what we discover 'through the study of motility, is a new meaning of the word "meaning".'[14]

Merleau-Ponty is describing the human being, with only a few references to other sentient beings. But it may be that his insight can be clarified if we begin with an example of an intense involvement between an organism and its environment in other species. We cannot be sure that the experience is identical, but at least it can serve as an analogy for the human commitment to the world. The phenomenon in question is well known: territoriality. But that word evokes a variety of meanings, perhaps none of which is of interest here. What we are concerned with is something that can seldom be asked by the biologist, namely what if *feels* like to have a territory.

Consider the case of a small fish like the stickleback,[15] which is commonly used as an example of territoriality. Normally size is of considerable importance to this creature – the largest usually prevails. But when the breeding season transforms the mood of the male, size does not guarantee deference. It appears that, once a small fish has established himself in a territory, he behaves very unrealistically and ignores physical size altogether. He even seems to forget what an insignificant specimen he is and will attack a much larger fish if it intrudes upon his territory.

In short, it is as if the boundary of what the fish considers to be *himself* has expanded to the dimensions of the territory. He regards himself as being the size of the territory, no longer an organism bounded by skin but an organism-plus-environment bounded by an invisible integument. The new boundary is not distinct, however. It is revealed as a gradient of action, with the fish becoming less liable to attack as distance from the centre increases. It is as if there were a kind of field in the territory, with the self present throughout but more concentrated at the core.

This is in striking contrast to the usual state of affairs, in which the fish is non-propertarian and acts as if it was indeed bounded by its skin. In this case there is more clearly an individual and an environment.

Now, if we take the admittedly precarious step of assuming some analogy, if not homology, between human beings and these more demonstrably territorial beings, another phenomenon becomes immediately apparent. Ever since Descartes we have been content to take the procedure described above a step further. Not only are we not a part of an environment, we are not even part of a body. We, the *real* we, is concentrated in some disputed recess of the body, a precious cocoon

separated from the world of vulgar matter. Far from extending our
self into the world as the territorial fish does, we hoard our ego as tightly
as we can. The narcissistic Descartes created 'a philosophy of solitude,'
and we suffer still from his success in 'drawing a set of rigid boundaries
around the *cogito*, [and] in withdrawing the ego from the world and
the body.'[16]

It has become apparent in the study of ethology that the extension
of self into setting is by no means abnormal or unusual. The idea that an
organism regards parts of its environment as belonging to its field of
self seems strange only when we begin with the assumption that visual
boundaries are more real than experiential boundaries. Our own
sensation of personal space gives us some insight into the nature of
self-extension, but of course the animal territory is not only larger but
constitutes a fluctuating field. That is, while the area immediately
around the self-centre may always be regarded as a part of the individual, the extension of that image to dimensions large enough for us to
notice and designate as territory varies with the mood of the organism.
What we see in territoriality is the visible manifestation of what each
of us goes through in sculpting a self. However, in this case we can see
the gap between the boundary of the body and the boundary of the
self. We cannot deny what we see in territorial animals, but our own less
visible commitment to an extended self is easier to neglect. Yet, each
of us is a part of the worldly action.

Such involvement with environment may seem unnecessary to some,
and indeed the evidence of attachment to objects has puzzled psychological theorists for some time. Most of these confine their attention to
the inner self; following Freud, they assume

*that the human being has a certain amount of love, called libido, which, at the
beginning, while remaining within the borders of its own self, is directed at its own
self. Later on in the development, actually from a very early state on, this love
detached itself from the self, it aims itself at things outside, which are therefore, in
a way, incorporated within us ... What we see is that the libido clings to things,
and that it does not want to give up things even if good substitutes are ready for it.
This is the grief, the sadness, about the perishing of things and of people.*[17]

But why should this occur? Why should the libido, the fundamental source of energy for the inner self, be expended on external things? Why should it not cling close to the subject itself? Contrary to this expectation, however, the 'energy partly detaches itself from the I and conveys itself to the outside objects.' The price we pay for this indiscretion is grief at the loss of the other in which we have invested this libidinal energy, this love or care. Freud's answer to this, the 'essential question of his psychology, and the essential question of the psychology of the twentieth century' in the opinion of J.H. van den Berg, is simply that the libido leaves the interior when the self becomes too full. Freud concluded that, 'in order to prevent it from being torn, the I has to aim itself on objects outside the self;' '"ultimately man must begin to love in order not to get ill".'[18]

Whether or not we accept Freud's explanation, it is significant that one so concerned with the inner man is forced to concede that there can be no such thing as a strictly inner man. Ultimately we must all invest ourselves in the world. And in many instances this investment is so profound as to make any distinction between the visible body and the loved other ultimately trivial. Far from a simple case of spillage, this is clearly the inevitable mode of development for sentient beings. Whether we refer to it as attachment to the other or as extension of the boundaries of the self, the fundamental fact of our existence is our involvement with the world. To return to Merleau-Ponty:

The world is not an object such that I have in my possession the law of its making; it is the natural setting of, and field for, all my thoughts and all my explicit perceptions. Truth does not 'inhabit' only 'the inner man', or more accurately, there is no inner man, man is in the world, and only in the world does he know himself. When I return to myself from an excursion into the realm of dogmatic common sense or of science, I find, not a source of intrinsic truth, but a subject destined to the world.[19]

The Cartesian Roadblock

In discussing the experience of being human Merleau-Ponty must deal with what is actually encountered rather than what is believed to occur. He deals with the experience of having a body rather than with the visible generic properties of bodies. Hence he must conclude that 'the objective body is not the true version of the phenomenal body, that is, the true version of the body that we live by; it is indeed no more than the latter's impoverished image, so that the problem of the relation of soul to body has nothing to do with the objective body, which exists only conceptually, but with the phenomenal body.'[20] There are two important points in this statement. One is that the phenomenal body is the one we live by; the other that the objective body exists only conceptually. This seems illogical, since we regard what is objective as being real. But of course it is the phenomenal body that we experience, that we live through, and the wonder is that we could ever regard it as unimportant. We all 'know,' however, that what is 'merely subjective' is always suspect, believing as we do that there is a separate and 'objective' world untarnished by human emotion. It is this belief that makes writers such as Merleau-Ponty seem inaccessible, and that makes speculations such as 'what does it feel like to have a territory?' seem inadmissible. We must therefore turn our attention to the origin of that belief, before we can proceed with our exploration of the relationship of mind to nature.

Earlier I have suggested that any society has a view of reality that is in some way restricted. Using the analogy of a photograph of reality from which a section is taken to stand as the whole, I have intimated that much that is of primary importance to the environmentalist is simply left out of the resulting official photograph. Schumacher's attempt at constructing new maps hinges on the inclusion of such features, and the introduction of the idea of a 'lived world' by writers such as Merleau-Ponty suggests a means by which the missing elements can be rediscovered. If we were to regard ourselves as 'fields of care' rather than as discrete objects in a neutral environment, our understanding of our relationship to the world might be fundamentally transformed. But to speak of such a transformation is to test the patience of any reader, for it is difficult to take seriously any claim for the discovery of a new reality. Nor, indeed, is that really what is being required here; rather it is an appeal to remember an old and ever-present reality, something we all experience and yet repress in favour of our cultural beliefs. Yet here again the reader may rebel, for none of us is normally aware of having such beliefs. Once they are firmly embedded and tacitly agreed to, unquestioned beliefs become what

Robert Combs calls 'the real authorities of a culture.'[21] They are the context in which we think, yet they are almost inaccessible. The biologist Jakob von Uexküll has claimed that a medium is invisible to an organism until it is removed from it: water is unknown to a fish until it discovers air. Our cultural medium is similarly transparent, and as a consequence we accept as common sense what persons in other cultures might find incredible.

This view conflicts with one of our most basic beliefs. The clash is inevitable, but it might be more comprehensible if we pause to consider a more modest instance of conflicting belief. In chapter 1 there was a brief discussion of the creation of new visual resources. So confident are we that we can recognize the beautiful in nature that we proceed to evaluate landscapes and identify those which merit preservation. Often the outstanding sites are mountainous. But had we conducted such a survey two centuries ago, the results might have been reversed. Marjorie Nicolson records a series of adjectives which testify to our ancestors' distaste for mountains. They are described as 'insolent, surly, ambitious, barren, sky-threatening, supercilious, desert, uncouth, inhospitable, freezing, infruitful, crump-shouldered, unfrequented, forsaken, melancholy, pathless,' not to mention 'such epithets as "Earth's Dugs, Risings, Tumors, Blisters ... Earth's Warts",'[22] and even 'Wens, Warts, Pimples, Blisters, and Imposthumes.'[23] Not even Pike's Peak escaped untarnished: 'The dreariness of the desolate peak itself scarcely dissipates the dismal spell for you stand in a confusion of dull stones piled upon each other in odious ugliness.'[24] Apparently the favourable response to mountain scenery is by no means innate. It is not at all obvious that certain kinds of landscape are beautiful. Rather, 'we see in Nature what we have been taught to look for, we feel what we have been prepared to feel.'[25] Nature, therefore, is different for different people in different times. Reality is transformed by what we are prepared to perceive. In the case of landscape beauty, it appears that we owe our preferences to those painters who first took it upon themselves to represent the landscape, and to show us what they discovered. It was not a case of the artist painting the beautiful but of the artist painting what he perceived, which was later defined as 'the beautiful.' The art historian E.H. Gombrich has observed that 'we call a scenery "picturesque" ... if it reminds us of paintings we have seen' and that 'the discovery of Alpine scenery does not precede but follows the spread of prints and paintings with mountain panoramas.'[26] When we are asked which landscapes are beautiful, therefore, we are not so much being asked to exercise our aesthetic judgment as to identify correctly those scenes which are of the type 'beautiful' – that is, those that were painted by earlier painters. In a sense, then, landscape beauty is a cultural artefact. This is not to suggest that there could not be a human response, even an aesthetic response, regardless of cultural influence. But the form the experience takes is biased by the foundations upon which we build. Reality is partly belief: we find what we intend to find in the world.

In this example it is the artists who constitute a significant influence upon our appreciation. As Oscar Wilde put it, the 'wonderful brown fogs' of London did not exist until art had invented them. This is not to suggest that the fogs did not occur, but no one noticed them until their qualities were revealed through art.[27] But the art of painting has itself undergone transformations as the nature of reality has shifted. One of the charms of landscape painting is its faithful impression of reality. In the Renaissance it became possible to depict the expanse of landscape in a more realistic way – or so we believe, we to whom 'looking real' is high praise for a painting. But far from struggling for visual accuracy, the creators of 'realistic' art, art reliant on linear perspective, strove for an ideal: geometrical perfection. Theirs was no homage to reality; it was homage to God, the great Geometer. It was an attempt to depict a perfect world, the world as it *ought* to be. 'Linear perspective, then, with its dependence on optical principles, seemed to symbolize a harmonious relationship between mathematical tidiness and nothing less than God's will. The picture, as constructed according to the laws of perspective, was to set an example for moral order and human perfection.'[28]

Prior to this time, the painter represented the world as he experienced it, not just as he saw it. Like a child, he was able to depict a qualitatively heterogeneous world. The child shows differences in value primarily through differences in size: the mother is usually the largest person in the scene, as befits her status. Heads are large relative to bodies, not because they are seen to be so but because they bear the most meaning. Even more mundane images, like buildings, will have important parts revealed, such as the door with a large knob to permit entry. Significance is incorporated into the image along with strictly retinal impressions. With his mastery of perspective the artist did not merely gain a technique; he lost many of his most valuable means of expression. Constrained to paint in a geometrically appropriate way, he had to find a new and subtle means of overcoming the sense of homogeneity that accompanies acceptance of uniform space. 'His perspective contruction was intended to copy no specific place. It provided a purely abstract realm which the viewer would discern as a world of order: not the beguiling, undisciplined world of the late Gothic International Style painters, but *real* space in the sense that it functioned according to the immutable laws of God.'[29]

The Renaissance artist is forced into a placeless world by virtue of the technique which he has embraced. The concept of a homogeneous world which is so apparent in science thus arose almost simultaneously in art. Qualitative variations are ignored in favour of geometric space, unencumbered by human distortion. In the service of an abstraction the artist represses his experience so as to display an ideal, an ideal which comes to be regarded as real. Whether the new technique of linear perspective is the source of or the response to a shift in attitude, the fact remains that at a particular time in a particular culture a new world emerges. For perhaps the first time the landscape of meaning is supplanted by the landscape of fact. Before the Renaissance human beings, like other creatures, occupied a qualitatively heterogeneous world, riddled with significant places. Only the offspring of the Renaissance have ever imagined it to be all the same, neutral matter for transformation and exploitation. This they have accomplished by scraping all traces of value from the environment and vesting it solely within the boundaries of the ego. The result is an aggrandizement of the individual human being and the creation of a bare and bleached environment. But, as we have seen, the experience of human beings does not entirely agree with this concept of reality. The phenomenal body is not strictly delimited; it is involved with the world. What does it mean, then, to attempt to live and create a self in a world devoid of significance? If the world is not just a backdrop but is rather the context of man, what does this change signify to the individual? How does

one sculpt a self out of a meaningless world? R.D. Laing warns us
that:

> *Our behaviour is a function of our experience. We act according to the way we
> see things.*
> If our experience is destroyed, our behaviour will be destructive.
> *If our experience is destroyed, we have lost our own selves.*[30]

It is no accident that Laing shares Merleau-Ponty's enthusiasm for
experience, for both of these writers have intellectual connections to the
philosophic tradition known as phenomenology. And phenomenology long ago encountered that cultural belief, alluded to earlier, which
today confronts the environmentalist as he reflects on the implications
of interrelatedness: both the phenomenologist and the environmentalist
collide with our assumption of the world as an accumulation of subjects and objects.

I have suggested earlier that both the discounting of experience as
merely subjective and the belief in an objective world separate from the
individual conspire to make such writers as Merleau-Ponty difficult to
comprehend at first reading. In effect, he denies that such a division is
meaningful at all. This is not to suggest that he denies the existence of
an external world, but he questions the reality of the division between
the self and the world. That division, in turn, is at least partly a
consequence of an important figure referred to earlier, René Descartes.

It is especially difficult to accept that the world we encounter was
formulated, at least in part, by other human beings. It is also difficult, I
suspect, for those of us in western societies, who value the man of
action so highly, to accept the influence of artists and intellectuals.
Ludwig von Bertalanffy, a biological theorist and originator of General
Systems Theory, once argued that such people are actually 'the hidden
marionette players of history – those who create world views, values,
problems, and solutions; in short, that symbolic backdrop against which
every scene of the great drama of history is enacted.' Their influence
is not limited to the ivory towers they are thought to inhabit but is
diffused throughout society so as to influence everyone. "The *Weltan-
schauung,* the view of life and the world, of the man in the street – the

chap who repairs your car or sells you an insurance policy – is a product of Lucretius, Carus, Newton, Locke, Darwin, Adam Smith, Ricardo, Freud and Watson – even though you may safely bet that the high school or even the university graduate has never heard of most of them or knows of Freud only through the *Dear Abby* column of his newspaper. It is we who, in the last resort, *manufacture the glasses* through which people look at the world and at themselves – little as they may know it, and little as they are aware of who it was who put the glasses on their metaphorical or metaphysical nose.'[31] Thus, it should not seem unreasonable to suggest that one man, Descartes, could so embody the spirit of his time as to have a lasting influence on the way we live our lives and draw our maps.

Descartes was an important catalyst in the precipitation of a new world-view, the one we commonly call scientific. There were important figures in science before Descartes, but it was he who spelled out most clearly the requirements and consequences of scientific thought. He saw it as his mission in life to establish an entirely new approach to knowledge. Today, we would probably think of it as analytic thought. But basic to it was an assumption of dualism.

Descartes set himself the task of discovering how to attain certain knowledge. It seemed obvious that man can easily be misled by superstition or faulty observation, but, even with care, how can we be sure that we are detecting the world as it is? How do we know it is not all an elaborate hoax? May not reality be non-existent? Perhaps there is only me, and all else is a dream. How can we ever be certain? But as he dwelt on this problem, doubting everything, it suddenly occurred to Descartes that there was one thing of which he could be certain: the fact that he was doubting. And if he was doubting, if he was thinking, then clearly he must exist. Finally, something certain: I think, therefore I am. And, since there are plainly two kinds of material in the world, that which can think and that which is thought of, subjects and objects, the famous dualism was asserted. The means to certain knowledge must be through systematic doubt. The thinking matter, the subject, must doubt what he perceives around him and reduce it to its basic parts. When he can reduce it no farther, his knowledge will be certain, and he will be left with 'clear and distinct' ideas all expressed in the language of certainty, mathematics.

The kind of analysis Descartes recommended and his reliance on mathematics are well known to us all. But what is of greater significance here is the assumption underlying this method, that of a basic division between thinking matter (*res cogitans*) and extended matter (*res extensa*). That there is the thinking subject, me, and all the things out there which I may know and use seems obvious. But it also raises problems. We still do not know why there should be any necessary correlation between what is in the mind and what is outside. Since they are entirely separate, how do we actually know there is a constant relationship? Mary Warnock concludes that 'the Cartesian problem thus can be seen to be that of relating what I am aware of to what there is; and of course this problem would not have arisen in this form if he had not insisted that the criterion of all knowledge was an internal criterion, namely that of the clarity and distinctness of our own mental content.'[32] Descartes builds a barrier between man and nature and invites us to guess what is on the other side. But as long as the guesses follow the given form, they are believed accurate. Each time we frame a guess which is then tested (subjected to systematic doubting), we edge closer to certainty. To put it in more modern terminology, each time we fail to disprove a hypothesis, the probability of its being accurate is increased and our confidence is fortified. The world constructed through science is a series of tested hypotheses. It is this 'world of guesses' that we are asked to adopt in preference to our own experience of the world. And we have. Alfred North Whitehead has referred to the seventeenth century as the 'century of genius,' primarily because of the contributions of Descartes and his successors, Locke and Newton. The outcome of their investigations was a new view of nature, but nature as 'a dull affair, soundless, scentless, colourless; merely the hurrying of material, endlessly, meaninglessly.' It was an enormously successful operation, and the view proposed

is still reigning. Every university in the world organises itself in accordance with it. No alternative system of organising the pursuit of scientific truth has been suggested. It is not only reigning, but it is without rival.

And yet — it is quite unbelievable. This conception of the universe is surely framed in terms of high abstractions, and the paradox only arises because we have mistaken our abstraction for concrete realities.[33]

This mistaking of abstractions, or guesses, for what is actually encountered in the world Whitehead calls 'the fallacy of misplaced concreteness.' We believe our guesses to be things. We believe everything to be things. And we act as beings existing in a clutter of things. In chapter 1 I have spoken of resourcism and the tendency to reify certain properties in nature so as to make them consistent with our beliefs about the world and amenable to scientific description. The aesthetic response to the world is thus transformed into a quantifiable entity, a visual resource. This is just a minor instance of the fallacy that Whitehead identifies, of mistaking a concept for a thing. More important, it results in our treating reality as an object rather than as an experience. Aesthetics is a way of being, a stance towards the world; an aesthetic experience requires a relationship between a seeking subject and a responsive world. But scenery is a stockpile of usable commodities.

Here again we begin to stray beyond what is acceptable, because we challenge a belief so fundamental as to appear unassailable. Of course there are subjects and objects, of course there is man and there are resources – it is obvious. Descartes made it obvious, and secured us from involvement in the world. In convincing us that the world is composed of distinct subjects and objects he insulated us from concern with the world and made it next to impossible for us to regard the world as anything but a storehouse of material. But Descartes was wrong.

That statement is certainly not new: Descartes's failings have been amply discussed in the philosophical literature. Yet public faith has never been shaken, for his ideas have achieved a separate existence. Criticism of Descartes therefore seems unrelated to our own expectations of the world. But we must confront those failings, for they obscure the need for alternatives. The societal maps that Schumacher challenged are tracings from Descartes's original, a map which excludes concrete experience of the world in favour of abstraction. The sense of separation which Descartes bequeathed to us may well be the most potent adversary of environmental thought. Our next task, therefore, must be to examine the tactics of others who have tried to challenge this dualism, to see if they offer us any means of conveyance beyond this conceptual impasse.

CHAPTER THREE

Returning to Experience

To the Things Themselves

The tools of the environmentalist spring from an understanding of the world that does not accord with his individual experience and does not even seem able to accommodate the goals he seeks. Some challenge to those assumptions about the world is clearly necessary, and yet even if a person accepts such a challenge, he is not likely to awaken to a new world tomorrow. Whatever the criticism, we shall not cease to perceive objects. But the objects themselves may be somewhat mutable. To the question, 'would the world contain objects as it does now, if all the conscious people were swept away?' Mary Warnock answers: 'it would do so in exactly the same way as it would continue to contain words and sentences after all the people had gone. What would be absent would be significance.'[1] The challenge to Descartes is, in part, a defence of significance.

The school of thought known as structuralism concerns itself with disclosing the innate tendencies of the human mind. One of these tendencies is said to be the formation of categories. This is simply a human way of coping with the world. For example, when faced with continuum of electromagnetic radiation that is detectable by the eye, we tend to break that continuum into describable units, which we call colours. The exact breaks may vary from society to society, with some recognizing only a few colours and others many. But all create such categories rather than dealing with the continuum as such. The structuralists go on to explain how symbols can be derived from these basic categories, so that traffic lights, for instance, may use red and green to signify opposite commands and yellow as an intermediate. In a much broader sense we could even say that life is a continuum that human beings see as a series of categories called species. And again there are differences in the number of divisions each society will make. Some will be content with a category called 'worms,' while others may insist on naming every breeding population as a separate unit. Inevitably it is the categories that come to seem most real, and the original continuum becomes an irrelevant bit of metaphysical nonsense. We identify 'regions' as things and regard those as real. Obviously, there are differences between these regions, and the categories are a useful shorthand, but saying there are differences or polarities is a far cry from saying there are absolute distinctions. And to question a particular duality is not to close one's eyes to differences but to open them to continuities.

Obviously we cannot avoid the creation of categories, any more than we can avoid the social construction of reality. The inclination to tell the story of 'how the world is' seems basic to being human. Indeed, the formation of categories may be important to the development of human capacities.[2] We can only hope that when the story turns out to be too far removed from actual experience to be reliable, we still have the skill to return to the world beneath the categories and re-establish our connection with it. It may be, in fact, that it was a glimpse beyond the categories of the day that inspired the Romantics to commend direct experience to their readers. And more recently it may be such an insight that has induced certain philosophers to advocate a return 'to the things themselves.' That phrase is connected with the tradition referred to earlier, which has the unfortunate and unwieldly name, 'phenomenology.'

That tradition originates with Edmund Husserl, a mathematician-turned-philosopher who was alarmed by the increasing application of scientistic thought to all areas of endeavour and the consequent foreclosing of other avenues of thought. Philosophy seemed to him to be especially compromised in this homogenization, for he felt that to accept the Cartesian dualism was to forfeit any chance of arriving at an understanding of persons in the world. Since his rise to prominence in the 1920s Husserl's ideas have been embraced (and transformed) by a variety of thinkers, some of whom are well known even in English-speaking countries. Sartre and other existentialists, for example, owe a considerable debt to Husserl. However, while North Americans may have only a passing acquaintance with this tradition, it has been much more widely adopted in Europe, where it can be regarded as the dominant philosophic school. We need not be particularly concerned with its academic lineage, however, beyond knowing that it has had fifty years of development and some renowned advocates. What is of special interest here is that it offers an illustration of how one might go about establishing an understanding of human-in-the-world which transcends the limits normally imposed by our Cartesian presuppositions. Indeed, it aims at avoiding presuppositions of any kind.

Actually, we have already been discussing the kinds of insight that flourish within the phenomenological tradition. The observations by Merleau-Ponty about our embodied existence admirably convey the flavour of this style of research. But the tradition that informs Merleau-Ponty's work also has much to say of the human commitment to the immediate environment and the world at large. That being so, it may also be able to provide more than a means of conveyance around the Cartesian roadblock. It may also speak directly to the concerns of the environmental movement, or at least some portion of it, for as Merleau-Ponty affirms, the goal 'is to understand the relations of consciousness and nature.'[3] In what follows we must try to move beyond the experience closest to us, that of the body, and consider too the experience of world and earth, without defining those terms further at this point.

Phenomenology is difficult to describe concisely. Describing it as 'an inventory of consciousness as that wherein a universe resides'[4] may be accurate but is not initially satisfying. Perhaps we may at first think of phenomenology as a kind of deliberate naïvety through which it is possible to encounter a world unencumbered with presuppositions. It is a formal resistance to the kind of reality-censorship practised by Galileo when he declared size and shape to be real, smell and colour unreal. Whatever is encountered simply is, without qualification. Phenomenology requires a return to the things themselves, to a world that precedes knowledge and yet is basic to it, as countryside is to geography and blossoms to botany. This seems initially confusing, for we think of knowledge as something achieved through observation and analysis, not as something which precedes it. Yet this notion presupposes an observer who surveys the world and questions it – the Cartesian view again. And this model of a passive receiver trying to gain knowledge of an external substance that emits signals is just what the phenomenologist refuses to accept. All that is admitted is experience. What causes it is not at issue; what it means is. The first requirement is not explanation but description.

Searching for a cause of perception seems a worthwhile project only if one assumes an isolated consciousness. But if you begin by rejecting that, the situation is quite different. A mental act is directed at its object and essentially includes it within itself: consciousness encloses its object. As Husserl says, consciousness is always consciousness *of*. There is no such thing as consciousness as an isolated entity, only consciousness of something – not even Descartes can just think. The object is inevitably built into the act of consciousness, and that which is perceived is not dependent solely on the object out there, but on the actual manner of grasping in consciousness. Thus, the division of the world into subject and object is trivial. The world is an ingredient of consciousness. Erazim Kohák offers a helpful example. Consider a man looking desperately for an ashtray:

After a few puffs, the subject looks anxiously for a place to deposit his ashes. There are no ashtrays. The subject casts about, settles on a seashell or a nut dish, and, with a mixture of anxiety and relief, knocks off the ash. He did not 'find' an ashtray 'in the objective world'; there was none there to be found. Rather, he constituted an ashtray in his act.

Common sense, in ordinary reports, passes over this and, instead of reporting, interprets *the experience as an encounter with an object out there in the world.*[5]

Notice that common sense finds a world of objects because it overlooks the act of consciousness and concentrates on an interpretation of what is experienced. Hence the thing identified always seems more central and more real than the act itself – the act remains effectively invisible, for it is not noticed. But to be ignorant of the act is to miss the very context of meaning for the object. Remember, the smoker's ashtray was not there at all until it was required. Yet the ashtray he believes he found was not imaginary either; it exists where it functions, in his experience. The ashtray depends on both the smoker and his world for its existence, for it can only *be* if there is a smoker who has a world. In R.D. Laing's concise phrasing, 'a person is the me or you, he or she, whereby an object is experienced.'[6] And, we might add, whereby significance is discerned.

At this point the relevance to environmental concerns may not be evident. But we must bear in mind that we are considering a different *starting*-point for examining those or any other concerns. This tradition implies that it is misleading to speak of an isolated self surveying a world, for the person is from the start *in* the world, and consciousness is always *of* the world. The world is the evidence we have of our own involvement. By shifting attention from the reality of the world, which Descartes was forced by his assumptions to attempt to prove, to the *meaning* of the world, phenomenology disposes of the distance between the thinker and his object. And given this different point of departure, one is free to ask quite different questions.

The actual methods of phenomenological investigation are as uncommon and initially puzzling as are its insights. And its task is especially difficult, for it must attend to experiences, and experiences are had by persons. We can study territory by observing subjects, but we may study experiences only by trying to become the experiencer.[7] Once a phenomenon has been selected for study, one must examine each occurrence of it with a view to grasping its meaning in the experience of the person concerned. To do that the investigator must put his own beliefs aside; he must 'bracket' his own preconceptions. It is not enough simply to observe the behaviour of another, for this will not reveal the meaning of the phenomenon. The example of the smoker is a fairly simple one, for even the non-smoker can comprehend the significance of a receptacle to the smoker. But the challenge of discerning the functioning of another's world is formidable, and the results are seldom dramatic. The accumulation of such descriptions is impressive, however, and even more so is the attempt to go beyond the description of the individual case to describe the meaning of such experience to humankind in general. In their broadest sweep phenomenologists give us an overview of the experience of being human. This may be done through specific examples of embodiment, as Merleau-Ponty demonstrates in his *Phenomenology of Perception*. Or it may be done as a direct project, an attempt to give a phenomenological description of being human. Such undertakings are attempted by few, and fully accomplished by none. But there have been some remarkable attempts, and perhaps none more impressive than the one to which we now turn our attention.

Hearing One's Name

Martin Heidegger is a controversial figure, admired by many and disdained by some. But whatever one's opinion of him, his stature is such that he cannot be ignored. Even as superficial a treatment as I offer here must reveal how very different our circumstances seem when approached through a radically different understanding of being human.

Heidegger was a thinker on a monumental scale. He did not dabble in trivial issues or write footnotes to the ideas of others. He strained to see as deeply as he could into the dark glass of existence, and with good reason. Heidegger was convinced that our way of thinking about the earth and ourselves had become seriously distorted. Essentially he argues that we took a wrong turn which has led us further and further from an understanding of our situation, and that no amount of remedial thought is going to set it right. We cannot correct our path by adding qualifications to existing assumptions. Instead, he believes that we must go back to the point at which the road divides and the wrong direction was chosen. This leads him to the site of that decision in ancient Greece. And the misunderstanding that stems from that decision entails nothing less than the question of what it means to be.

At first glance this question seems alternately trival and meaningless. Being is something we take so completely for granted that it seems unnecessary to spend a minute, much less a lifetime, reviewing it. We know that we are, we exist, and that beings are just other entities that we encounter and learn to master. But this is our first misconception, for the fact of being is far from trivial. After all, Heidegger asks, why is there something rather than nothing? What does it mean to exist? What does the verb 'to be' really mean? What is 'is'? We use that word incessantly, without realizing that we do not know, in any but the most superficial way, what it means. Laing tries to demonstrate its importance thus:

'The sky is blue' suggests that there is a substantive 'sky' that is 'blue'. This sequence of subject verb object, in which 'is' acts as the copula uniting sky and blue, is a nexus of sounds, and syntax, signs and symbols, in which we are fairly completely entangled and which separates us from at the same time as it refers us to that ineffable sky-blue-sky. The sky is blue and blue is not sky, sky is not blue. But in saying 'the sky is blue' we say 'the sky' 'is'. The sky exists and it is blue. 'Is' serves to unite everything and at the same time 'is' is not any of the things that it unites.

None of the things that are united by 'is' can themselves qualify 'is'. 'Is' is not this, that, or the next, or anything. Yet 'is' is the condition of the possibility of all things. 'Is' is that no-thing whereby all things are.[8]

We deal quite comfortably with the concepts of 'sky' and of 'blue'; these human-defined categories are interpreted as tangible things. But look what we take for granted: 'is.' Without the 'is,' nothing else matters. The most remarkable part of the statement is not that the sky is blue, but rather that the sky *is*. That is astonishing. Why, after all, should there be something rather than nothing? It is far easier to ignore this question than to confront it. And having taken being for granted, we can simply attend to the details: the blueness and the sky-region. Yet we cannot *entirely* take it for granted, for at some level we are inevitably aware of this incredible possibility, of being or not-being.

Heidegger treats this as a virtually diagnostic feature of being human – the awareness of the possibility of non-being. Our own mortality makes that unavoidable, much as we may try to side-step it. But there it is: not only might we not have been, but we were not, and we will not be. We are a temporal phenomenon, a momentary flash of being soon to fade to non-being. But what might the consequences of that flash be, however brief? What might it illuminate? What is revealed through the circumstance of human being? And what is the significance of there existing a creature for whom Being is an issue? In his *A Sand County Almanac* Aldo Leopold observes that, had we become extinct, the passenger pigeon would not have mourned us. It could not, for it could not grasp the significance of our demise. Only in a creature like ourselves can the significance of extinction be realized. Mind you, it frequently seems that we do our best to avoid such realization, but,

according to Heidegger, the frequency of such avoidance was not always
so great. Attention to Being was eclipsed in the time of Plato, and
from that time forth our single-minded preoccupation with beings has
dramatically altered our understanding of the world and ourselves,
and has jeopardized both. Heidegger proposes that we set aside this
prejudice and pause to think it through again.

Given the conclusion that we became forgetful of Being a very long
time ago, it is apparent that we have been building on inadequate
foundations ever since. And thinkers like Descartes are the inevitable
culmination of a 2500-year-old stream of thought. Once our 'forgetfulness' had taken hold, it was only a matter of time until its consequences
were thought through and the world-view implied by it was made
explicit. 'I think, therefore I am' may seem a significant insight, but it
avoids a more important one. Descartes took for granted the verb. He
concludes: 'I *am*' – but what does it mean to be? 'With the "*cogito sum*"
Descartes had claimed that he was putting philosophy on a new and
firm footing. But what he left undetermined when he began in this
"radical" way, was the kind of Being which belongs to the *res cogitans*,
or – more precisely – the *meaning of the Being of the "sum"*.'[9]
Heidegger tries to reverse this, with predictably puzzling results. For he
must attend to that which we ignore, and for which we have no
common words. Most of those which might once have served his purpose have gradually been eroded to 'thing' terms. Even phenomenon,
which meant '*that which shows itself in itself*, the manifest,'[10] is now
regarded as a 'thing that appears or is perceived.'[11] This constitutes a
significant change:'"*phenomenon*", the showing-itself-in-itself, signifies
a distinctive way in which something can be encountered. "*Appearance*", on the other hand, means a reference-relationship which is an
entity itself.'[12] Such distinctions are vital to Heidegger's project and
make it necessary for him to choose his words with great care. This
makes it difficult to paraphrase his insights, for the terms he uses seldom
relate exactly to colloquial expressions. However, with the necessary
vocabulary established, Heidegger is able to attend to Being rather than
to beings. But that too poses a challenge to his reader, for his is a
project with which we have little or no previous experience.

Earlier I suggested that we might try to think of a tree with the
visible presence removed, so that only actions and relationships remain-

ed. In a sense this is just what Heidegger attempts with respect to humans: he dissolves the body and describes the event. In fact, he does not even refer to 'man' in his classic *Being and Time* – to do so would have defeated his purpose. No thing-terms may be used, nothing to distort the description. If one imagines trying to describe the acts of personhood – the moods, relationships, understandings, anxieties, and so forth – without reference to a material housing or visible object, one can appreciate the difficulty of his undertaking. Essentially Heidegger tries to give us a phenomenological description of human being – he gives us the 'essence' of how we are. This is a monumental project, and one which he made no pretense of having accomplished. But he made a provocative beginning by describing us as a being for whom Being is an issue and whose way of relating to the planet is through 'care.'

In reading Heidegger one does not so much follow an argument as encounter a new yet familiar world. It is, after all, ourselves he is describing, yet us from the inside, us as the experience of being rather than as the thing called humankind. Once the nature of his task is understood and the terminology absorbed, the description is compelling. But as George Steiner warns: 'to "understand" Heidegger is to accept entry into an alternative order or space of meaning and of being.'[13] The alternative is sustainable only within Heidegger's terminology; when we return to our more comfortable 'thing-language,' the images congeal immediately. Even terms that are nearly synonymous are apt to solidify without warning. Earlier I used the term 'field' to try to avoid speaking of distinct objects. It is useful, for we have experience of magnetic fields in which there is clearly 'something going on,' and yet nothing tangible or visible. But this too can be turned into something more solid, a kind of bubble around the magnet that stands for lines of force and soon becomes more line than force. However, if we could conceive of a 'field of care' or 'field of concern,' we might have a means of gaining partial understanding of Heidegger's description of human being. His term is not 'field,' however; it is *'Dasein'* ('Being-there' in German), and 'the Being of Dasein itself is to be made visible as *care*.'[14] We know a territory by the actions of its occupant; we know *Dasein* by the evidence of care.

One of Heidegger's interpreters, William Barrett, offers an especially useful description of how it is to be such a field of care.

Now, there is nothing at all remote or abstract about this idea of man, or Dasein, as a field. It checks with our everyday observation in the case of the child who has just learned to respond to his own name. He comes promptly enough at being called by name; but if asked to point out the person to whom the name belongs, he is just as likely to point to Mommy or Daddy as to himself — to the frustration of both eager parents. Some months later, asked the same question the child will point to himself. But before he has reached that stage, he has heard his name as naming a field or region of Being with which he is concerned, and to which he responds, whether the call is to come to food, to mother, or whatever. And the child is right. His name is not the name of an existence that takes place within the envelope of his skin: that is merely the awfully abstract social convention that has imposed itself not only on his parents but on the history of philosophy. The basic meaning the child's name has for him does not disappear as he grows older; it only becomes covered over by the more abstract social convention. He secretly hears his own name called whenever he hears any region of Being named with which he is vitally involved.[15]

Notice that this is not unlike a suggestion considered earlier, that one does not really experience the boundary of the self as the epidermis of the body, but rather as a gradient of involvement in the world. But instead of considering the extension of the self into the world as akin to the making of a body image or a 'phenomenal body,' here we are talking about a field of concern or care. The child recognizes the primacy of relationship, that its parents are an intimate part of the event that is itself. This may not be altogether unlike the experience of persons who are moved (often to their own surprise) to defend the useless, non-human world around them. Each 'secretly hears his own name called whenever he hears any region of Being named with which he is vitally involved.' Whether it is the housewife who defies the chainsaws to rescue a tree that is beyond her property yet part of her abode, or the elderly couple who unreasonably resist expropriation of their home, or the young 'eco-freak' fighting to preserve some vibrant, stinking bog, or even the naturalist who fears the extinction of a creature he has never seen, the phenomenon is similar: each has heard his own name called, and reacts to the spectre of impending non-being.

The Saving of the Earth

Thus far we have seen how the intuitions of the lived world are given form through phenomenology, and how the non-Cartesian project of Heidegger provides us with an alternative understanding of ourselves in the world. But while this understanding may help clarify the kinds of observations reported in chapter 2, the relevance to the environmentalist may still not be apparent. Of course, any alternative may be useful in helping us see our condition in a different light, but this particular one has been singled out by some as being especially appropriate to the environmental movement. To see why, we need to remember that *Dasein* is not just a different way of saying 'man,' but represents a different concept of being human, a 'field of care.'[16] And being such a field means more than being a body; it means being-in-the-world, and it also implies a different sense of environment.

Although humans have a bodily existence just as other creatures do, and are similarly reliant on the earth, they also have a particular aptitude: they inhabit what Heidegger calls 'world.' World is that part of earth which is open to human understanding. Heidegger says it is 'that "*wherein*" a factical Dasein as such can be said to "live",'[17] and that worldhood is 'that referential totality which constitutes significance'[18] (the very feature which Warnock claimed would vanish if conscious people were swept away). World may refer to the public 'we' world or to one's private environment. But above all it is the realm of the understandable, our region of significance and meaning. In world we are surrounded by the knowable and the 'ready-to-hand.' There are ashtrays in world where there are only surfaces and recesses in earth. World is filled with instruments of use, and with significant places. It is not a random assortment of objects but has a structure that is apparent to us. John Wild, while not speaking specifically of Heidegger, offers a helpful summary:

when I enter the room I do not first have to count up the separate objects to know where I am. I must first grasp the region as a whole before I can grasp the places of the different implements. Each region is for something, and points beyond itself to further regions. Taken together, they point to an ultimate object of care, for the sake of which they all are. This is that ultimate horizon which I call the world, *and within which I myself and all the beings I know are now located. Wherever I go, my world goes with me. Without a world-field surrounding him, there can be no human person.*[19]

If we fail to understand that Being-in-the-world is a state of *Dasein*, then we shall of course overlook the existence of worldhood. Indeed, we shall try to interpret what we encounter in terms of the 'present-at-hand,' which we may loosely describe as the merely present, or the 'objectively' existing things of the world. These are not things with which we have any involvement, and therefore they are not entities we encounter in world. If we understand nature as a collection of neutral things, then 'this manner of knowing them has the character of depriving the world of its worldhood in a definite way.'[20] But if, on the other hand, we encounter it as a part of our lives, as something with which we live and as 'equipment' which we live through – as something 'ready-to-hand,' in other words – then the Nature we encounter will be quite different.

Here, however, 'Nature' is not to be understood as that which is just present-at-hand, nor as the power *of Nature. The wood is a forest of timber, the mountain a quarry of rock; the river is water-power, the wind is wind 'in the sails'. As the 'environment' is discovered, the 'Nature' thus discovered is encountered too. If its kind of Being as ready-to-hand is disregarded, this 'Nature' itself can be discovered and defined simply in its pure presence-at-hand. But when this happens, the Nature which 'stirs and strives', which assails us and enthralls us as landscape, remains hidden. The botanist's plants are not the flowers of the hedgerow; the 'source' which the geographer establishes for a river is not the 'springhead in the dale.'*[21]

If we encounter nature as natural resources, then we deny it any of the character of worldhood. And we simultaneously deny ourselves access to it as home. It is characterized by space, not by place. There is no human involvement and therefore no sense of significance in such a nature. Julian Marias, writing in a parallel vein, although not specifically of Heidegger, asks:

Is it true that the two hundred thousand species of coleoptera form part of the natural world? We have to say definitely not. They do, if you like, form a part of nature, which is nothing more than an interpretation of the real, performed by some men, that is, by the naturalists. Those species would be, perhaps, ingredients of the world of the naturalist, but not the world of man as such. They are not, strictly speaking, component parts of the world, *as are, in contrast, automobiles, telephones, ships, trains ...*[22]

Marias must exclude the thousands of beetles from world because they do not have the character of worldhood – they do not *function* in the lives of most humans. This is not to say that they could not, or should not, but that they do not. Nor can they ever, if they are stripped of significance through designation as mere presence-at-hand. The botanist's plants are neutral objects; the flowers of the hedgerow function in the life-world of the human. They are significant.

Of course, our contemporary bias is to emphasize mere presence-at-hand, and our nature is almost exclusively 'natural resources.' According to Heidegger, this is a bias which is heavily reinforced through technology. Again, however, one must bear in mind that the meaning of Heidegger's terms is often unique, and technology to him is not simply the creation and utilization of tools and techniques. It is rather the encountering of the world as a field *for* the use of tools. As a way of revealing, technology shapes our understanding and limits our possibilities. It gives us nature as a 'standing reserve' and makes us the operatives of this vision.

Only to the extent that man for his part is already challenged to exploit the energies of nature can this revealing which orders happen. If man is challenged, ordered, to do this, then does not man himself belong even more originally than nature within the standing-reserve? The current talk about human resources, about the supply of patients for a clinic, gives evidence of this. The forester who measures the felled timber in the woods and who to all appearances walks the forest path in the same way his grandfather did is today ordered by the industry that produces commercial woods, whether he knows it or not. He is made subordinate to the orderability of cellulose ...[23]

The understanding of the world that technology requires of its functionaries ensures that nature can only be encountered in this way. It also ensures that, ultimately, people will be encountered in the same way, as the present-at-hand. But it is not simply that we need modified techniques to achieve an 'appropriate' technology, or even that we have made imprudent management decisions concerning the use of technology; we do not 'use' technology in that sense at all, but are its functionaries. We live through it rather than with it. And it is probably inevitable that we do so. 'It is precisely because exploitative technology and the worship of allegedly objective science are the natural culmination of Western metaphysics after Plato, that the Heideggerian summons "to overcome metaphysics" is, simultaneously and quintessentially, a summons "to the saving of the earth". The two are indissoluble.'[24]

This observation by George Steiner both summarizes the dilemma and gives a hint as to why Heidegger is regarded by many as an important figure in environmental thought. Even though his concern is almost exclusively with humanity, the understanding he brings to his subject points to a radically different relationship between humans and earth. His appeal to environmental advocates is understandable in the light of statements like the following:

Mortals dwell in that they save the earth – taking the word in the old sense still known to Lessing. Saving does not only snatch something from a danger. To save really means to set something free into its own essence. To save the earth is more than to exploit it or even wear it out. Saving the earth does not master the earth and does not subjugate it, which is merely one step from boundless spoilation.[25]

If we compare this with statements by the 'deep ecologists' described in the first chapter, the similarity is striking. Even allowing for Heidegger's idiosyncratic use of terms, there is no doubt that his admonition to the saving of earth is germane to the environmental movement. Joseph Grange has used his insights to suggest a 'foundational ecology' that 'seeks the ground of our relation with nature as well as its corresponding depths in the human psyche.'[26] And he suggests that Heidegger's illumination of body, world, and earth helps delineate the role such a foundational ecology should play.

Can we summarize these intricate relations of earth-body-world within the meaning of foundational ecology? What is most concrete in all our investigations thus far is this: that in our human being we want nearness to that which distances itself from us. We seek to be the neighbor of that which withdraws from the light of openness. Yet that neighbor, the earth, and even our body, gives itself without cost and without price, freely of itself to us — if we but respect it and let it be what it is. Ecology is therefore learning anew to-be-at-home *in the region of our concern. This means that human homecoming is a matter of learning how to dwell intimately with that which resists our attempts to control, shape, manipulate and exploit it.*[27]

Such a homecoming is obviously incompatible with the attitude of dominance and exploitation that is entailed in technology. In everyday life we have the experience of being '*Dasein*-with' other persons, and of being '*Dasein*-in' a world. But at times we realize, as Steiner observes, that we must also be '*Dasein*-for'; and '*Sorge*, signifying "care-for", "concern-for and -with", is the means of this transcendance.' It is also the basis for an 'existential ethic of concernedness' from which derives 'Heidegger's subsequent definition of man as the shepherd and custodian of Being.'[28]

To mention ethics in an environmental context is to encourage reminiscences of Aldo Leopold's celebrated 'land ethic' and to raise hopes that some behavioural credo can be established to restrain us from dangerous excesses. But Heidegger offers no easy manifestos. Instead he says: 'if the name "ethics," in keeping with the basic meaning of the word *ēthos*, should now say that "ethics" ponders the abode of man, then that thinking which thinks the truth of Being as the primordial element of man, as one who eksists, is in itself the original ethics.'[29] Understanding ourselves is the first task of ethics, and the ethics we derive will depend on our understanding of Being. There is no possibility of an environmental ethic, then, in a society dominated by the technological vision of the world.[30] Consequently, Michael Zimmerman concludes that 'Heidegger holds that appropriate ethical limits can only arise within a new *ethos*, a new paradigm for understanding what we and other beings *are*.'[31] And an understanding of ourselves and others is the fundamental task of thinking.

Sacred Horror

In effect, Heidegger has changed Descartes assertion, 'I think, therefore I am,' into something like 'I care, therefore I am.'[32] In doing so he has accomplished just what is necessary for a rethinking of environmentalism. He removes the Cartesian roadblock and opens the way to everything excluded from the societal maps that Schumacher has challenged. All those important things that cannot be spoken of until they are measured are now returned to their place of honour. And the illusion of an unconcerned, dispassionate human master is replaced by a totally involved agent of Being. The notion of isolated individuals inhabiting a neutral environment is similarly dismissed. We do not have an environment until we have a world. Max Scheler has claimed that 'to find one's place in the world, the world must be a cosmos. In a chaos, there is no place.'[33]

As we mentioned at the outset, the phenomenological method requires an attempt to divest oneself of expectations so as to observe what is simply given. Anything of which we are aware is a datum of experience and worthy of note. However, the method itself is of less interest to us than is the rejection of assumptions that the method entails. Merleau-Ponty admits that the atoms of classical physics will continue to seem more real to us than our own experience, 'as long as the attempt is made to build up the shape of the world (life, perception, mind) instead of recognizing as the source which stares us in the face and as the ultimate court of appeal in our knowledge of these things, our *experience* of them. The adoption of this new way of looking at things, which reverses the relative positions of the clear and the obscure, must be undertaken by each one for himself, whereupon it will be seen to be justified by the abundance of phenomena which it elucidates.'[34] The well-known revelations which figure prominently in the making of the environmentalist may be understood as a triumph of experience over belief, of the concrete over the abstract. The Romantics made such experience famous, perhaps even trite. But it is never trite to one who encounters the world in its overwhelming solidity. Steiner claims that 'it is hidden Being that gives the rock its dense "thereness", that makes the heart pause when a kingfisher alights, that makes our own existence inseparable from that of all others. In each case, wonder and reflection tell us of an intensity of presentness, of an integral unfolding of self-statement, *clearly in excess of sensory data and neutral registration.*'[35] This bringing forth of Being from conceal-ment Heidegger calls 'alethia' or truth – not truth as we now mean it, not as correctness or as an impression matching an original, but as a revelation of inwardness. John Muir experienced this in encountering the small plant *Calypso borealis*, as did Justice William O. Douglas before a chinook wind, and David Brower in the Berkeley Hills.[36] These events, minor though they may seem, were profoundly important to the individuals involved and, indirectly, to the environmental movement in general. For it was the experience of a concrete reality that precipi-tated their rejection of societal convention and their advocacy of a different relationship with the natural world. Heidegger's philosophy has been called one of 'radical astonishment.'[37] Some of his insights were doubtless known to these naturalists who were liberated by wonder. And they have certainly been known by poets, and perhaps never more explicitly than in Coleridge:

Hast thou ever raised thy mind to the consideration of EXISTENCE, *in and by itself, as the mere act of existing? Hast thou ever said to thyself thoughtfully,* IT IS! *heedless in that moment, whether it were a man before thee, or a flower, or a grain of sand? Without reference, in short, to this or that particular mode or form of existence? If thou hast indeed attained to this, thou wilt have felt the presence of a mystery, which must have fixed thy spirit in awe and wonder. The very words, There is nothing! or, There was a time, when there was nothing! are self-contradictory. There is that within us which repels the proposi-tion with as full and instantaneous light, as if it bore evidence against the fact in the right of its own eternity.*

Not TO BE, *then, is impossible:* TO BE, *incomprehensible. If thou hast mastered this intuition of absolute existence, thou wilt have learnt likewise, that it was this, and no other, which in the earlier ages seized the nobler minds, the elect among men, with a sort of sacred horror. This it was which first caused them to feel within themselves a something ineffably greater than their own individual nature.*[38]

The talent of *Dasein* is awareness of Being and astonishment at what is. But the other side of the coin, as Coleridge indicates, is the awareness of the possibility of not being, and the consequence is the anxiety that characterizes so much of our existence and which leads to such crippling attempts at denial. But we cannot, ultimately, ignore what is implicit in this awareness, this stepping back from Being: the 'essential homelessness of man.'[39] Heidegger once observed that 'University philosophers will never understand what Novalis said: "Philosophy is strictly speaking a homesickness".'[40]

One is moved to philosophize when one does not feel at home anywhere. Such activity may reassure us, but it never succeeds in completely alleviating that fundamental anxiety. But our homelessness is not of significance only to ourselves. It is of vital import to life on earth, for our behaviour as placeless beings is a factor in the lives of all. Heidegger says relatively little in a direct fashion about other creatures, but by describing us to ourselves he opens the way to an understanding of our consequences to others. And it is to those consequences that we must now turn, for of course the aspirations of the environmentalist cannot be addressed exclusively through examination of ourselves and our culture, any more than they can be addressed without such understanding. The issue is ourselves among others, and we must now look to that broader picture before returning to the question of homelessness.

CHAPTER FOUR

A Biology of Subjects

Objects, Facts, Feelings

We have now traced the source of the environmentalist's failure to a tacit understanding of reality that is incompatible with the acceptance of the existence of value in nature. We have also seen how an alternative trend in western thought seeks to transcend the limitations imposed by the conventional view, and in so doing leaves open the possibility of seriously addressing the concerns of the environmentalist. But our attention thus far has been focused exclusively on the cultural attributes of humans, and particularly on the varying views of reality which can be accommodated by consciousness. There has been no assertion of a basic human mind-set, nor even a suggestion that there is a single correct view of the world to which we should aspire. Of course, we normally assume that there is a correct version, usually our own, and environmentalists can be as sanctimonious as anyone else in defending their views. But if nothing else, phenomenology should alert us to the perils of assuming that there can only be one 'right' version of reality. Criticizing the dominant paradigm does not necessarily indicate a desire to provide a particular substitute. Nelson Goodman once noted that in making such criticism one may seem to be in alliance with mystics and others who reject the scientific world-view. But there is no such alliance, since the mystic would set up his own version of the way the world is, while the phenomenologist is intent on resisting the adoption of any single way. There are many ways the world is, many facets of reality to be explored. And it is through discovering as many of these ways as possible that one achieves an approximation of the world. 'For me, there is no way which is the way the world is; and so of course no description can capture it. But there are many ways the world is, and every true description captures one of them.'[1]

Phenomenologists speak of 'intentionality,' referring to the mind's ability to point beyond itself to an object, and of 'constitution,' meaning our ability to impose an interpretation upon an object (and so a receptacle becomes an ashtray). These properties of consciousness ensure that whatever is perceived is not neutral, not just the passive reception of external stimuli, but the result of our active involvement in grasping the world. This makes the strictly objective world a fiction. We cannot postulate one class of perceptions which is real (measurable) and another which is fanciful (value, meaning, mood). All derive from the same source and are equally valid experiences of the world. Factual beliefs are not simply deductions from objective study; they 'are educed, that is, drawn out, as what is latent becomes manifest. They are educed from the only world I can observe, the world as perceived, the world as constituted.'[2] That world is the life-world.

The term 'life-world' may suggest a biological context, although this is not particularly the connotation its users would expect. Most phenomenologists who concern themselves with human existence, and particularly those who also share the views of the existentialists, would probably wish to avoid any connection with biology. But as we shall see, there are strong parallels between Husserl and at least some biological theorists. Before discussing these, however, I should caution the reader that I am using the adjective 'biological' in a slightly unusual sense. Most of the authors involved would indeed describe themselves as biologists, but their range of speculation goes well beyond the norm for that discipline. They do not confine themselves to the mechanical aspects of living things, nor to features that have obvious 'survival value.' They are interested in the methods of self-maintenance that are the concern of biology in general, but beyond that they also comment on the nature of the lives they study, including animal consciousness. We might say that they engage in a biology of subjects as opposed to the more conventional biology of objects, for they certainly do not treat the creatures they study as mere pieces of behaving matter. But this is not to suggest that their work is somehow less accurate than that of their more pedestrian colleagues. For our purposes it might be more useful to describe their work as an ecology of subjects, and as such it yields a different kind of information than does most ecological research. An ecology of objects gives us energy budgets and photosynthetic efficiency ratings, while an ecology of subjects gives us a world replete with such invisible features as territory, place, and the elusive 'compliance.'[3] And these, in turn, tell us a great deal about the involvement of a living being with its environment.

In chapter 3 we considered the dualism we have inheritied from Descartes, and some attempts to overcome it. It may be well to bear in mind, lest we place all the blame (or credit) on Descartes, that we apparently all share some predisposition to dualistic thought, at least in so far as we think in categories. I have mentioned the structuralist assertion that the tendency to create categories is universal in human beings, and that it easily leads to an assumption that the categories which one names are actually discrete objects.[4] The example used was light, whose range of wavelengths is broken into separate units called colours. The number of these categories may vary from two to many, but the act of breaking the continuum into fragments is universal. I have suggested that this may be observed in almost any taxonomy, and that even the spectrum of life forms is made to seem more a collection of things (species) than it need do. Furthermore, our understanding of any phenomenon is generally hampered by a restriction in the number of categories recognized. Those cultures which recognize only two colours cannot have the same degree of colour sophistication that we do, any more than we have anything approaching the understanding of snow that the Inuit demonstrate with their range of terms for snow. The greater the range – that is, the finer the distinctions we make within the spectrum – the more subtle our knowledge of the world. The more ways of the world that are recognized and described, the closer our approximation of the essence of the phenomenon in question. But in the most important case of all we choose to deny ourselves any subtlety of knowledge whatever. For what Cartesian dualism amounts to is a description of the continuum of being in just two categories: thinking matter and extended matter – or, more colloquially, 'us' and 'it.' Everything in between is not simply ignored but defined as impossible.

No degree of intermingling is allowed: there is only the self and the other, never self-and-other, or extended self, of a field of care, even though we all have direct experience of these rather than of complete separation. Now, it may be that such concepts as personal space are evidence of the inadequacy of this dualism, and of our effort to overcome restriction by naming intermediate positions without formally recognizing them. Nevertheless, the overall effect is to deny the individual any insight into the gradient of self which radiates throughout his world. In accepting this dualism we agree to remain ignorant of our degree of involvement and interrelatedness. The consequences are well known to philosophers, although many choose to disregard them. Heidegger cannot, of course, for it is this diminished understanding of Being that constitutes his starting-point. And his discussion, like that of most phenomenologists, is in large part a detailed rejection of Descartes. Indeed, this must be the starting-point of anyone who challenges the notion of total separation and who asserts a belief in literal interrelatedness. This is a debate the environmentalist participates in as well, though seldom explicitly.

I have suggested earlier that whatever claims ecology may have to being a genuinely subversive science must rest upon literal interrelatedness, something conventional ecology begins with but quickly forgets. For the very notion of interrelatedness contradicts the Cartesian premises which biology, in seeking to be scientific, readily accepts. Hence, there is a substitution or re-interpretation effected whereby 'interrelated' is taken to mean 'causally connected.' The two terms may sound similar, but they reflect different beliefs about the nature of relationship. To say that you are related to your sister is not the same as saying that you are causally connected to her – even though, in the eyes of a devout mechanist, it may seem so (the so-called selfish-gene hypothesis effectively interprets all interactions as ribonucleic narcissism). But relatedness also implies a set of non-physical bonds of commitment, obligation, affection, and so forth – all qualities which exist through living beings, and between them. If we choose to acknowledge such things as these, we effectively join the biologist Adolph Portmann in reversing Galileo's categories of the primary and the secondary (or the authentic and inauthentic in Portmann's terms). For Galileo what is real is that which would still exist with the living being removed. In contrast, Portmann regards the whole range of perceptible phenomena, those which would not be possible at all but for the existence of living creatures, as 'authentic.' And those phenomena on which Galileo would place primary emphasis because of their independence of living beings are, for Portmann, 'inauthentic.'

Portmann, perhaps more explicitly than any other contemporary biologist, returns the subject to centre stage in biological thought. He often does so in the course of treating material more casually handled by others, such as territoriality. What may be an interesting sidelight to some, or something whose survival value must be explained, is to Portmann indicative of an important breakthrough in the way we think of animals. 'The realisation that territory is a biological fact has helped to obtain full attention for the subjective spheres of owning and defending it, and has made the most subjective thing of all, the individual's experience and social impulses, a field for new objective research.'[5] Marjorie Grene, who has done a considerable service in bringing the work of Portmann and other European biologists to the attention of the English-speaking public, adds that 'this frank avowal of the existence of the *subject*, not simply as a fringe phenomenon, but as the object of scientific research, may have ... far-reaching consequences for our thinking about nature, about science, and about ourselves.'[6]

It is difficult to understand how such a mild-sounding assertion can be considered revolutionary. Why should studying subjects cause such an upheaval? We get a sense of the significance of this change only if we understand that it has been the practice to insist on a study of objects. Animals are not treated as subjects – and therein lies one of the reasons that we are often offended by comparisons between ourselves and other animals. 'Animal' is, by convention, the name of a thing, an object, a clever machine. To say one is animal-like is to say that he is thing-like, a mere object, or that he behaves like a machine, with no awareness or initiative. Of course, it is equally insulting to the animal. One of the simplest ways of defending the notion of absolute distinctions between human and non-human life is to encourage total ignorance of animals – a practice religiously followed by many humanists. Science also helps perpetrate such ignorance, paradoxically, because it gives us a mechanistic image instead of experience of the animal. So long as we have limited direct experience of the creatures in question, it is relatively easy to accept a cultural stereotype in its place, in this case animal-as-object. But when there is personal experience, a much more difficult substitution must take place. The student who enters a biology program with experience of animals as subjects must 'unlearn' his initial understanding before he can proceed to a biology of objects. The environmentalist, as an amateur in the best sense,[7] is never given such remedial work in world-perception, and so he finds continuing incongruity between his own understanding and that required by the environmental manager and the developer alike. Benefit-cost analyses can never include authentic phenomena in Portmann's sense of the term, however much they may pretend to. They are an exercise which entails the shuffling of cultural 'image-cards,'[8] but they cannot deal with an experiential reality. I recently listened to a nuclear technologist express horror that a court of law should recognize the legitimacy of residents' fears concerning the location of a nuclear plant. All that should be considered are 'the facts' – that is, the probabilities of nuclear accident as determined by responsible people (scientists); to be influenced by people's feelings and fears, he said, is dangerous. There are facts – probabilities – and there is garbage – feelings. One is real, one is not; one is reliable, one is dangerous. All this said with mounting emotion, of course, as he felt his position challenged. I expect we all know what he means by 'facts' and we probably agree, at some level, that they are real. But how can we possibly permit the assertion that our fears are less real or less relevant, when it is these we must live with and these which colour our entire existence? How can we permit this reversal of the primary and the secondary, our own direct experience of the world and an abstraction about it which for most of us really amounts to second-hand information? Why is the gossip of experts more real than immediate experience? This brings us back again to our Galilean world, but perhaps the significance of Portmann's challenge is now more obvious.

While Portmann may be the most visible advocate of a biology of subjects, he cannot be said to be the first, or the most read. We must return to his work presently, but it might be helpful to refer to an earlier figure in biology who, whether he actually influenced Portmann or not, did lay the groundwork for this kind of speculation. He was a contemporary of Husserl's, and the two have more in common than their time of publication (although as far as I know neither makes reference to the other). I am speaking of Jakob von Uexküll, considered by some to be the father of modern ethology.

Space versus Place

In an essay published in English von Uexküll begins by differentiating himself from those who regard animals as 'mere objects. The proponents of such theories forget that, from the first, they have overlooked the most important thing, the *subject*.'[9] He then goes on to describe the animal-subject and in his major work, *Theoretical Biology*, to devise a virtually new branch of study, replete with its own jargon. Fortunately, von Uexküll was not without skills as a popularizer, and although some of his images may seem a bit quaint, they often convey the author's meaning much more adequately than the complex phrases of Husserl or Heidegger.

Von Uexküll asks us to imagine that we are walking through a meadow and that we discern 'a soap bubble around each creature to represent its own world, filled with the perceptions which it alone knows. When we ourselves then step into one of these bubbles, the familiar meadow is transformed. Many of its colorful features disappear, others no longer belong together but appear in new relationships.'[10] In short, we step into a completely new world, but a world unimaginable to the mechanist with his belief in animals as automatons responding to stimuli rather than as subjects who help create their own worlds. All that a subject perceives becomes its 'perceptual world' and all that it does becomes its 'effector world.' Together these form a closed unit, the *Umwelt* (this is von Uexküll's term for the world of the individual organism). What he is asserting is the existence of parallel universes (*Umwelten*) within the world of living beings.

Von Uexküll's term *Umwelt* is still found in academic literature. So too is one of his illustrations, that of the world of the wood tick. The tick is literally and figuratively blind to the world as we know it. Most of what we perceive about our environment would be unknown and unknowable to the tick, and irrelevant – it has no need for mountain scenery. That sky is blue or grass green, that fresh earth smells thus and birds sound like that, all this is nonsense to the tick. If you could communicate

your belief in such a world to it, it would of necessity call you a liar.
For it knows the world is not that way at all. By our standards the tick
cannot see or taste, and even its sense of smell and touch must seem
perilously impoverished. But there are three elements of the planet
which it can perceive and rely upon.

A general photosensitivity of the skin leads the mature, fertilized
female to the top of the bush, to which she clings. What she needs to
complete her life cycle, her destiny if you will, is a blood meal from a
mammal. After that she can drop to the ground, lay her eggs, and die.
And the approach of the essential meal is heralded by the smell of
butyric acid – sweat. On receiving this invitation she executes her
ambush, dropping onto what should be a mammal. If she lands on
something warm, she feels her way to a relatively hairless spot and
indulges in the drink of life, for which she may have waited as long as
eighteen years. Now, just what she is drinking is unknown to her. If
one were to substitute warm water for blood, she would detect no
difference. There is no need to, for in her world warm, smelly persons contain the meaningful, essential fluid. What it tastes like is irrelevant – it is only supposed to come in one flavour.

The most interesting part of this story is that such a creature is able to
exist in a seemingly deprived world of only light, sweat, and heat. The
world of the tick is basically a set of gradients of those significant
features. To speak of reflexes and instincts is to obscure the essential
point that the tick's world is a world, every bit as valid and adequate as
our own. There is a subject, and like all subjects it has its world. All
animals, simple or complex, 'are fitted into their unique worlds with
equal completeness.'[11] The tick is able to occupy a world that is perceptu-
ally meaningful to it. Out of the thousands or millions of kinds of
information that might be had, the tick sees only what is of significance
to it. The world is tailored to the animal; they are entirely complementary. To define a tick as a creature with such-and-such a world would be
as precise a definition, if we could accomplish it, as the taxonomist's
careful enumeration of leg-hairs or mouth-parts. The subjective world
or *Umwelt* of the species is as unique a part of that creature as any of
its visible (that is, morphological) components. The animal does not have
a world-view; it *is* a world-view. And that world is as invisible as its
feelings, thoughts, emotions, reveries, and so on – all the things that lead

E.F. Shumacher to suggest that 'life, before all other definitions of it, is a drama of the visible and the invisible.'[12]

This is quite a different view of existence from our usual one in which the animal is simply an exploiter of certain natural resources. We are not talking just about observable interactions between subjects and objects but rather about a very complete interrelation of self and world, so complete that the world could serve as a definition of the self. Without the tick there is no tick-world, no tick-space, no tick-time – no tick-reality. This is a creature which can sit 'daydreaming' for up to eighteen years, waiting for the meaningful smell that will beckon it to a resolution. Time was never more obviously an organic phenomenon than here, where the creature can pass years as we might pass minutes. Indeed, the entire eighteen-year wait may well be experientially shorter than an hour in a dentist's chair. And of course human-time is equally unique. Maurice Merleau-Ponty emphasizes that 'the world is in-separable from the subject' and that we must say of time that 'it has meaning for us only because "we are" it. We can designate something by this word only because we are at the past, present and future. It is literally the tenor of our life, and, like the world, is accessible only to the person who has his place within it, and who follows its direction.'[13]

Much the same can be said of space, which is similarly organism-dependent. Rather than simply occupying space, an individual takes his place in a world. This place, as Grene points out, is defined not just by geography but by roles and responsibilities as well. Nor is she confusing space and place, for 'place is prior to space.'

This is not a confusion, but a recognition of the priority, in experience, of the concrete to the abstract. The child's dawning awareness of his body as his and of its localization at the center of things and events moving identifiably around it – it is this primary spatialization, so to speak, which underlines all spatial concepts, physical, geographical, mathematical, or what you will.[14]

Space is a part of the world of the subject – not the homogeneous space proposed by classical physics, but the qualitative mosaic which we know as individuals. This heterogeneity of worlds was part of what von Uexküll wished to portray, but he too had to confront the Galilean monolith with its extra-organic reality: 'We are easily deluded into assuming that the relationship between a foreign subject and the objects in his world exists on the same spatial and temporal plane as our own relations with the objects in our human world. This fallacy is fed by a belief in the existence of a single world, into which all living creatures are pigeonholed.'[15] Reality is inevitably a component of organic being, not something separate from it. As the tick illustrates, the world is a set of characteristics that has meaning for the organism in question. Von Uexküll was insistent that we recognize this proliferation of 'soap bubbles,' if only so that we realize that 'there is no space independent of subjects.' In addition, discerning the multitude of realities around us may help us 'recognize the soap bubble which encloses each of us as well.'[16] And when we recognize that, we are well on the way to understanding what Husserl had to say about ourselves and our life-world, for there is a fundamental similarity between the two perspectives.

The world we believe we inhabit would be nonsensical to the tick, for it is a human world which exists only for us. The 'life-field,' as John Wild calls it, depends on the organism that shapes it and gives it meaning.[17] But while the human condition is essentially the same as that of other beings, there is an important difference, of degree if not of kind. The *Umwelt*, according to Husserl, is constituted within an attitude or *Einstellung*. The world will change, therefore, with the mood of being. But the range of those attitudes is given in the nature of the organism, in what von Uexküll called the *Bauplan*, whereas in humans it is given in *consciousness* and is therefore much more variable.[18] We have, as Wild says, 'freedom of world-formation.' Hence the rainbow of cultural realities we encounter.

The essential similarity in the insights of these two writers, one dealing with organisms in general and one with humans in particular, is interesting and important. But for our purposes it may be the difference between their respective subjects that is most relevant, for the possibility of world-formation is of great importance, both in understanding what has happened and in estimating what may be possible. Perhaps we get a better sense of how great our ability to occupy different worlds is, and how subtle are the changes necessary to effect a transformation, if we examine one of the most obvious and apparently neutral aspects of perception. Whether the illustration that follows is anything more than a useful analogy is open to debate. Certainly it is only one factor, and singling it out may seem to amplify its importance. But, in any event, a brief examination of the nature of our most trusted revealer of reality, vision, may serve to emphasize the importance of human flexibility of world-formation, and the way in which minor distortions can come to have great significance to our way of understanding reality.

The Despotism of the Eye

In an essay entitled 'The Nobility of Sight: A Study in the Phenomenology of the Senses' Hans Jonas provides a provocative illustration of the interplay of biological and cultural factors. Given our available means of perception, it is apparent that the way our senses present the world to us influences the overall understanding of it we finally acquire. And if we place special importance on the evidence of one particular sense, then the influence of that kind of understanding will predominate and strongly shape our world. The world we accept is largely a consequence of our reliance on sight – or at least on a particular kind of sight.

Each sense is unique in some respect of course, but sight does seem singular. Vision provides access to the world in a particular way, and while it gives us much, it also conceals. 'The unique distinction of sight consists in what we may provisionally call the *image*-performance, where "image" implies these three characteristics: (1) *simultaneity* in the presentation of a manifold, (2) *neutralization* of the causality of sense-affection, (3) *distance* in the spatial and mental senses.'[19] While another sense, such as hearing, will give us information about what is going on around us, it is of a different nature. It can give us an indication of events occurring but not an instantaneous impression of everything surrounding us. Once the noise stops, the event ceases to exist and the listener is alone. Neither can the animal let its ears 'wander' as it does its eyes – it cannot survey the landscape the way it can through sight. Furthermore, the predominant sounds may not be the most important ones – they are simply those that seize the attention. And since sounds are not arrayed for the selection of the hearer, comparison is extremely difficult. Indeed, sound does not even indicate the existence of particular beings, except by inference. The bark of a dog is not the dog, but an event which we know indicates the existence of a dog. Hearing 'is related to event and not to existence, to becoming and not to being. Thus hearing, bound to succession and not presenting a simultaneous coordinated manifold of objects, falls short of sight in respect of the freedom which it confers upon its possessor.'[20]

When we think of reality, it is the evidence of vision that we embrace. Sight, with its simultaneity, neutralization, and distance constitutes a unique influence on the way we think. The fact that all is given simultaneously and in mutual proportion allows us to make objective comparisons. It would seem, then, that our cherished achievement, objectivity, may not be a discovery or a consequence of logical thought so much as the outcome of our reliance on one mode of access to the world. It is only because of this distortion in the ratio of sensory influence that we find ourselves in the world that we do. Vision permits us the luxurious delusion of being neutral observers with the ability to manipulate a distant environment.

The gain is objectivity, but the loss is any notion of interrelation between the elements of the visual field. We see only what is, not how it came to be. To vision the world is not happening but has happened; all we witness is the debris of existence. And accepting visual evidence as the most real, we find ourselves living in a world of things, in which beings are real while Being is mysterious. According to Jonas, 'the mind has gone where vision pointed.'[21] It may be that the writers considered significant in the establishment of the contemporary world-view were themselves the inevitable consequence of this sensory dependence. Certainly, as John Hanson has observed, Descartes's idiom was vision: 'The Cartesian idiom is filled with visual oppositions, the most famous being the "clear and distinct" against the "dark and obscure." Similar expressions suggest that, for Descartes, discourse, thinking, and even existence were essentially visual in nature.'[22] He further suggests that the famous aphorism 'I think, therefore I am' might equally well have been 'seeing is believing.' In a sense, then, the revolution in thinking which we associate with Descartes and others might, with some justification, be regarded not as an intellectual break-through but as a deliberate perceptual distortion. As we come to think only with the eyes, so to speak, a different world unfolds, a world which, as it turns out, is much more amenable to manipulation and control that was the older construction from a balance of senses.

Thus, it would seem that there has been a shift in the relative importance we attach to the information given us by the various senses, and that the evidence of vision is now given greatest credence. Just how this came to be may never be known, although suggestions such as those by Marshall McLuhan about the role of technology in amplifying the effect of vision deserve serious consideration.[23] But there is some measure of agreement about when this shift in emphasis took place, for there is evidence of the change. Around the time of the Renaissance, man became an individual. C.S. Lewis concludes that the medieval model of space provided the feeling of looking in on the world, whereas modern man feels that he is 'like one looking out from the saloon entrance on to the dark Atlantic, or from the lighted porch upon the dark and lonely moors.'[24] This is the attitude reflected in the new techniques of painting, which centre on the illusion of infinite space created through the invention of perspective. Such paintings reveal a world seen from the viewpoint of a single individual, the significant centre before which the world unfolds. And it is noteworthy that at about this time the first autobiographies appeared, again suggesting a new understanding of the significance of the individual. This also implies the annexation of value and truth to the individual, whose reflections now become the source of wisdom in place of the external world. Now, rather than searching in nature for meaning, one seeks the truth in other persons. Man becomes the measure of all, for he now believes himself to *be* all that is important. Once meaning is confiscated by a single source, the world is devalued, transformed into an empty vessel containing materials for human use.

Two events occur simultaneously, for they are two sides of the same coin: the human becomes the measure of all things, and the world becomes nothing but a collection of things for us to measure. Of the birth of the individual Lionel Trilling says:

The impulse to write autobiography may be taken as virtually definitive of the psychological changes to which the historians point ... at a certain point in history men became individuals.

Taken in isolation, the statement is absurd. How was a man different from an individual? A person born before a certain date, a man – had he not eyes? had he not hands, organs, dimensions, senses, affections, passions? If you pricked him, he bled and if you tickled him, he laughed. But certain things he did not have or do until he became an individual. He did not have an awareness of what one historian, Georges Gusdorf, calls internal space. He did not, as Delany puts it, imagine himself in more than one role, standing outside or above his own personality; he did not suppose that he might be an object of interest to his fellow man not for the reason that he had achieved something notable or been witness to great events but simply because as an individual he was of consequence. It is when he becomes an individual that a man lives more and more in private rooms.[25]

The rooms are private in more than the physical sense. There are private rooms in the self as well. Indeed, it is this division of self that Sartre refers to when he claims that 'by the distinction between the "id" and the "ego" ... Freud has cut the psychic whole in two.'[26] Thereafter, the individual is able to regard himself as an object of investigation, an object for which he (the ego) need not accept responsibility. When it is discovered within, animality can be disclaimed, relegated to the world of the external for dissection, examination, and evaluation by the *real* self. By withdrawing to this lofty vantage-point, separate not only from the world but also from the worldly portions of one's own being, the omnipotent ego peers out on an infinite world of matter and finds it wanting.

A new geometry is created in recognition of the central importance of the individual – or, some might argue, in preparation for the emergence of the individual. For with the invention of perspective a new way of seeing emerges that is consistent with the central role of the individual. Perspective 'insists on the single point of view' and hence is itself 'a mode of perception which in its very nature moves toward specialism and fragmentation.'[27] The adoption of this new way of seeing is of singular importance, reinforcing as it does the sense of detachment from the world: 'It is only perspective which allows for dispassionate survey and noninvolvement in the world of experience.'[28] The detached view increasingly relies on vision, the least intimate of the modes of extension. The adoption of perspective and the consequent reliance on visual assumptions have been said to have 'marked the effectual beginning of the substitution of visual for tactile space awareness' and thus initiated a different way of regarding the world and our place in it.

sight has today become the principal avenue of the sensuous awareness upon which systematic thought about nature is based. Science and technology have advanced in more than direct ratio to the ability of men to contrive methods by which phenomena which otherwise could be known only through the senses of touch, hearing, and smell have been brought within the range of visual recognition and measurement and thus become subject to that logical symbolization without which rational thought and analysis are impossible.[29]

There is, then, a constant amplification of the role of visual assumptions by translating more and more of our experience into forms accessible to them. Nor is this restricted to science and technology. Even in popular culture there is a constant encouragement to visual thinking. The consumption of images by industrialized societies is astonishing, and it is accompanied by pressure to make images and so to experience the world as pictures. In her book *On Photography* Susan Sontag observes that 'through photographs, the world becomes a series of unrelated, freestanding particles' and that 'the camera makes reality atomic, manageable, and opaque.'[30] Her comments could just as well constitute a critique of vision, and her thesis could have been that photography encourages visual thinking and staring as a way of life. In view of this, her suggestion that 'the habit of photographic seeing – of looking at reality as an array of potential photographs – creates estrangement from, rather than union with, nature,'[31] is significant. Visual dependency, so often encouraged as a source of nonconsumptive uses of wilderness, may be a part of the mental state that makes the task of the environmentalist so difficult.

However, it may seem to be going too far to link environmental concern to habits of sight. Surely we cannot argue that seeing is ultimately harmful? After all, we are certainly not the only creatures who can see, nor even the only ones who place strong emphasis on sight. But vision illustrates the way in which a property of the perceiver, even something believed to be neutral and non-distorting, can nevertheless strongly shape the reality encountered. The world we inhabit is partly shaped by the tools by which we know it. But what of those who share our visual abilities? Do they not derive the same benefits, and pay the same price? To address this, we need to begin with a few comments about the uses of objectivity.

Vision and Objectivity

In a sense objectivity has been an implicit feature in much of what we have discussed up to this point. It is not a simple term, although I am using it in the colloquial sense of that which is uninfluenced by personal feelings or motivations. To be objective, in this sense, is to be uninvolved – to be the neutral observer who is believed to be the most reliable guide to action. Since by this understanding the objective person is not personally committed, he has no vested interest in that which he views. Neither does he have any obligation towards it. He is totally apart. Now while we may admire this stance as a means of gaining information, we normally do not appreciate it as a way of gaining information about ourselves. That is, we do not enjoy having someone examine *us* objectively, and there is great suspicion of the objective professional. Going to a physician or a psychologist is a very disconcerting experience, not just because it is strange or unknown, but because it is deeply offensive. Consider what it means to be treated as an object.

We spoke earlier of the process of changing something into an object, such as changing a particular landscape into a resource. This conversion of a person, place, or idea into a thing can be termed 'reification' – a useful term, but one which can also have more specialized meanings in political theory. The frightening thing about being turned into a thing is that the person who does this to you need no longer treat you as a person, and so does not have the obligation towards you that you would normally expect. You are deprived of his kinship, and are therefore open to his manipulation. In treating you as an object he frees himself to do with you what he wills; all restrictions are lifted. This sounds rather despotic, something most people would not wish to do. But it may be that we are all so inclined, for in objectifying the other person we are also freeing ourselves from the fear of being objectified. Subjects have this power – they can objectify; objects are harmless. This may be the implication of some existentialist thought. The geographer Yi-Fu Tuan observes that 'things do not challenge man's subjectivity: they are domesticated, comfortable objects, barely heeded because they have no existence outside the human purview. Man's abuse of nature, whether it is to smother an animal in affection or to kill it for science, is easily understandable from the position of existentialism.'[32] This requires some elaboration.

The ability of the other to reduce one to the status of an object is readily observed in human interactions. Tuan uses the example of a man who believes himself to be alone in a room, and who suddenly becomes aware that he is being watched. 'At that instant he becomes self-conscious; that is to say, he sees the room and the things in it, including himself, from another's viewpoint. He has suddenly been deprived of his subjectivity and has become an object in someone else's world.'[33] And his response is anger and embarrassment, stemming from the change of state from a worldly subject to a worldless object.

If we try to consider this in the light of the involvement of self and world discussed in chapter 3, it does not seem particularly strange. There is probably some level of fear in all of us, of which we are seldom if ever conscious, that the other person has the power to destroy us, not physically, but in the sense of depriving us of the power that goes with being a self-willed centre of existence. To be observed is to be present in another's experience as a datum of the world, a thing among others in the visual panorama. Our only defences against this threat are to act quickly to assert our subject-ness through speech and action or to withdraw from sight.

Inevitably, in something so basic to daily existence there is a variety of expression, including some variants which can only be regarded as pathological or as 'disturbances in man's communication with the world.' Erwin Straus, another of the writers whom Grene discusses, has described some aspects of the disorders of 'looking at' in an essay on shame. With respect to the voyeur, he says:

In viewing, there is a transition from the immediate I-thou encounter, i.e., mutual participation, to a unilateral intention – a transition from the I-thou relationship to the subject-object relationship proper. All looking and being looked at is a lapse from immediate communication. This is demonstrated in everyday life by our annoyance and irritation at being observed ...

Thus, the voyeur does not participate in reality in any direct sense but only by way of the objectifications, i.e., reflected knowledge. He makes the Other into an object in and for itself.[34]

Straus considers shame the barrier between the public or objectifying function exemplified by the voyeur and the 'immediate being' which requires a strict reciprocity between the persons involved. Being ashamed is an indication that the important barrier between public being and immediate being has been breached and that the latter is threatened. Thus, far from being the anomaly some psychiatric authorities have believed it to be, shame must be regarded as 'an original feature of human existence and shamelessness as acquired behavior.'[35] But for our immediate purposes the more interesting of Straus's insights is that '"looking at" objectifies.' The detached observer, the stranger or the voyeur, does not participate. On the contrary, he keeps his distance, for 'objectification is only possible with a keeping of distance, and, conversely, it is only the keeping of distance that makes objectification possible.' By insisting on this lack of involvement in his knowing of the world, the voyeur distorts his understanding. According to Straus, 'he makes the Other into an object in and for itself.'[36] And all of us resent and fear this transformation.

An angry response to being looked at is not uncommon, nor is it restricted to humans – although the extreme which Straus describes may be. Mary Midgley singles out the fear of being looked at for special attention in her study *Beast and Man*. She points out that being stared at provokes unease or anger in a variety of species, many of which regard the stare as an open threat of aggression. Consequently normal social relations often have to proceed with elaborate avoidance of direct eye contact.

To stare steadily while you approach someone, or to stand still staring after he has seen you, is as direct a threat as can be made. Why *this should be so is an interesting field for inquiry. It may well have something to do with the fact that predators naturally stare fixedly at prospective prey before jumping on it. And they are of course regarding it as an object, not as a possible friend – which is just the effect a direct stare conveys to a human being.'[37]*

Whatever its origin, this is so widespread a phenomenon that many creatures are able to use it to their advantage, even those that lack the ability actually to stare. Many insects, for example, have developed eye-like spots on their bodies which can be flashed to unnerve a vertebrate predator. Roger Callois has described a wide range of such phenomena in *The Mask of Medusa*, and he claims that evidence of the trans-specific importance of the staring eye can be deduced from its use by humans in art and design.[38] Being stared at is a significant event. It is 'not just a threat. It constitutes an actual intrusion.'[39]

Midgley notes that the stare is especially characteristic of the predator, and suggests that our response may stem from that connection. But while this may seem a simple biological explanation and one consistent with selection theory, we must bear in mind what is involved in the act of predation. Predators, or at least social predators, are extremely inhibited in the expression of aggressive and dangerous behaviour. They do not attack readily, for there are elaborate restraints pervading their lives, restraints which apparently prevent the predatory mood from arising in inappropriate circumstances. A social predator like the wolf will not harm its kin. It will not harm those whom it knows as subjects, those who are 'like me.' What may be involved in the act of predation is the objectification of the prey. Only when the animal is stripped of subject-ness, of any vestige of kinship, can it be regarded as an object for predation. The first stage in predation is therefore objectification, the second is pursuit, and the third is the consummation or the breaking off of the chase. But that first stage is vital, both in view of the observed effect of the stare, and of the many observations of predator-prey 'conversations.' The latter are difficult for us to credit, given our view of predators as killing machines and of prey as innocent victims. But events such as those reported by Barry Lopez in *Of Wolves and Men* are not uncommon.

In the preceding section on hunting I merely touched on that moment of eye contact between wolf and prey, a moment which seemed to be visibly decisive. Here are hunting wolves doing many inexplicable things (to the human eye). They start to chase an animal and then turn and walk away. They glance at a set of moose tracks only a minute old, sniff, and go on, ignoring them. They walk on the perimeter of caribou herds seemingly giving warning of their intent to kill. And the prey signals back. The moose trots toward them and the wolves leave. The pronghorn throws up his white rump as a sign to follow. A wounded cow stands up to be seen. And the prey behaves strangely. Caribou rarely use their antlers against the wolf. An ailing moose, who, as far as we know, could send wolves on their way simply by standing his ground, does what is most likely to draw an attack, what he is least capable of carrying off: he runs.

I called this exchange in which the animals appear to lock eyes and make a decision the conversation of death. It is a ceremonial exchange, the flesh of the hunted in exchange for respect for its spirit. In this way both animals, not the predator alone, choose for the encounter to end in death.[40]

Whether or not one accepts Lopez's interpretation of a 'ceremonial exchange,' it is difficult to discount the possibility of some sort of communication. If we rephrase his observation in the language of the preceeding discussion, we might argue that what is under discussion is the state of the prey's being. The wolf stares: objectification is inevitable, unless the prey can resist and effectively deny the wolf's accusation. Those eyes shout out 'thing!' But the prey must not let that interpretation bounce back to the wolf. Instead, it must show itself as a centre of existence, a wilful presence which asserts its subjectivity and therefore its kinship with the accuser: I am not a thing; I am a subject like you and you must afford me the rights and respect that our kinship requires. Such an assertion during the 'conversation of death' will suppress the mood of predation and force the predator to assume its normal stance as a social being with reciprocal obligations to other beings. But should the prey be unwilling or unable to present itself as a subject, then object it must be. Like the human who becomes aware of another watching him, the prey must either display its self or retreat from sight – or suffer the consequences of expulsion from the society of living beings.

Normally this conversation results in a mutually agreed-to mood and actions appropriate to it. Instances of deviance from the norm, of predator overkill for example, seem always to be related to some impediment to perception. Weather or darkness may obscure the communication, as may the inbreeding which has made domestic animals functionally illiterate. Such an animal has already forfeited all but the rudiments of subject-ness anyway, and would have little to say even if it had the means to express it. Indeed, according to Erazim Kohák, 'deprivation of freedom is equivalent to destruction of subjectivity.'[41] He is speaking of humans, of course, but his observation may be more generally valid. The domesticated animal is a creature stranded in a foreign world, a world of which it can never 'make sense.'

Perhaps the consequences of the 'stare of objectification' are most easily illustrated in a phenomenon we witness and hear of almost daily. An enormous portion of our population is all too familiar with the consequences of the stare, and publicly laments its treatment as a 'sex object' – an entirely appropriate term. Women understand this phenomenon very well. When the visual imperative they provide evokes the unrelenting gaze of the male, there exists an intensified version of what we all experience under the scrutiny of the other. Once again, the options are retreat or asserting one's personhood, that is, the use of speech and action to make the male acknowledge the presence of a subject rather than just an object. This is normally successful, so long as the means of this conversation remain unimpaired. In small communities this can be accomplished very effectively, since all persons are to some degree acquainted with each other as subjects. The woman has a relatively easy task in reminding her companion of their shared status as subjects and community members. But in at least two instances, big-city living and pornography, the conversation is thwarted and the woman at risk. There is no way in this situation to remind the male of the woman's subject-ness. In both these instances the woman is anonymous. She has no name; she is not a person. She has no past to recall in support of her claim, and in the case of pornography she has not even the power of speech by which to demonstrate her subject-hood. Her defences are removed as completely as those of the domes-ticated animal. Remember Straus's injunction: '"looking at" objectifies. Objectification is the second and essentially perverse action of the voyeur, along with his keeping his distance.'

What is odd, then, is not the human being's ability to objectify or the role of staring in it. Many animals can temporarily occupy an objective world, a world of things. But they quickly return to the normal mood, to a world born of a balance of senses. There is little fear of any one mode gaining the upper hand, for the corrective to objectivity is built in. In fact, we may consider calling the ability to assert one's subject-ness a fundamental property of all animal life. This may essentially be what Portmann describes with his properties of 'display' and 'centering.' As Grene translates them, display is 'life's showing of itself on the surface,'[42] while centricity, 'inseparably allied to but contrasted with display, consists in the fact that organisms are *centers* of perceptions, drives and actions.'[43] Animals behave as 'centers of doing and letting be,'[44] and they declare their existence to the world – even ones that live such obscure lives that no one is apt to experience their performance.

Particularly in the so-called higher forms, such as social mammals, the visible displays of selfhood are of great importance. Such animals are, Portmann reminds us, 'in many ways distinguished by strong social emotions, by an intensive communal life. It is possible for simple sensory stimuli to keep animals together in swarms; but it is hardly anything more than mere crowds which are gathered together in this way, so long as there is no mutual expression of moods so that the being together is raised to a richer relationship, to a true meeting of independent creatures.'[45] It is the mutual expression of moods with which we have been concerned, and which prolonged objectivity destroys.

That we have been so successful in prolonging our periods of existence in a state of objectivity is remarkable, but perhaps a cause for concern rather than applause. Certainly it cannot be considered just a biological failing, an overdevelopment of visual perception. A quick review of the history of ideas will serve to remind us how hard we have worked to accomplish this, and the calls for more expertise and more objectivity in the management of the world should serve to remind us that the pressure to objectify is still very strong and probably growing. But again biology and culture cannot be separated, and what one does is often amplified by the other. If we can trace our skills in objective thought to the imperatives of vision, perhaps we can also see evidence of this reliance on vision as reinforcing the cultural strictures. That is, perhaps we not only derive objectivity from vision, but reinforce it as a cultural norm through culturally encouraged reliance on one style of vision. Maybe we 'see' too much.

Seeing without Staring

I have referred earlier to Susan Sontag's discussion of photography, and her assertion that it has served as a cultural force encouraging estrangement from the world. But she goes still further, effectively describing photography as a promulgator of voyeurism. 'Taking photographs has set up a chronic voyeuristic relation to the world which levels the meaning of all events.'[46] If true, this could indicate that such visual technologies act as amplifiers of our already large prejudice in favour of the visual, and distort still further the shape our society will take. Perhaps photography encourages even more staring at the world, with the usual consequences. But even if this is so, there are surely differences within photography, some approaches being more analogous to staring than others.

If we confine ourselves to 'nature' photography in the broadest sense, this variance is fairly apparent. We have animal photography which is plainly predatory, often practised by men who were once hunters in the more usual sense and who bring a similar approach to their photography. But at the other extreme we find a much less objective kind of photography practised by a few dedicated artists. Landscapes such as those achieved by Ansel Adams, Wynn Bullock, Paul Caponegro, George Tice, and Edward Weston are far from literal renderings and can perhaps more accurately be described as place portraits. While Sontag may be right in suggesting that photography encourages detachment from the world, there are probably qualitative differences within the medium that should discourage any blanket condemnation of photography (or of vision). The comments that follow are simply a further illustration of the alternative worlds open to persons with different sensory balances. Even within an apparently visual medium there is the possibility of transcending the purely visual. It is possible, in other words, to see without staring.

But staring is strongly encouraged by the medium of photography, and even by the equipment itself. It may be significant that the most revealing place portraits were done some years ago, before the technology changed and the single-lens reflex camera became the norm. Any change of instrument, of mechanical appendages, brings with it some alteration in stance as well. Initially, the camera required a high level of involvement on the part of the photographer. He had nothing we would call a viewfinder, and therefore had to find the picture with his mind before trying to re-create it on film. Once committed, he set up his apparatus, often including a portable darkroom, and proceeded to create and then expose his photographic material ('film'). By judicious choice of position, lens, filter, exposure, and development, he could occasionally possess a template through which to re-create the mental image that had precipitated his arduous enterprise. There was nothing casual about this activity at all, and the photographer was more akin to a sort of image-gardener than to the glass-eyed predators we see portrayed in camera advertisments today. And, judging from the comments of successful landscape photographers, the attitudes were as different as the equipment.

Such photographers placed the 'self at reality's service.' For them a great photograph was 'a full expression of what one feels about what is being photographed in the deepest sense and is, thereby, a true expression of what one feels about life in its entirety.'[47] The photographer was said to project 'himself into everything he sees, identifying himself with everything in order to know it and to feel it better,' or to be like 'a Zen archer, who must *become* the target so as to be able to hit it.'[48] Their immersion in their activity was total, partly because of their goals and partly because of the involvement required by their equipment. But even minor changes, such as the addition of viewfinders to hand-held cameras, precipitated changes in attitude.

When the viewfinder became common, there were two alternative types to choose from (three, if we consider the ground-glass back of the camera on a stand to be a kind of viewfinder). One option was the now-standard 'eye-level' viewfinder, the other a 'waist-level' device with a separate viewing lens and a ground-glass which the photographer could study by looking down. Even today there are arguments between proponents of these two types, for, strange as is may seem, there is a difference not only in the style of operation but in the results obtained. The eye-level device allows one to operate as if the camera were an extension of the photographer, and with his new eye he can fix a recording gaze on anything at all. But the waist-level camera changes the approach of the photographer to the subject. In this case the camera is not an extension of the photographer's eye. It is rather more like carrying a small projection box, on whose screen various compositions magically appear. But perhaps most significant, in light of our earlier discussion, the photographer with this type of camera does not stare at his subject. In fact, he effectively bows to it. There is no subliminal threat whatsoever, and subjects seem to respond accordingly. Without the anxiety of objectification, subjects relax and work of extraordinary honesty and power can emerge. The work of such artists as Diane Arbus and Bill Brandt bears witness to this, and anyone who has experienced the two instruments will have felt the difference.[49] But both photographer and subject experience something subtly different in the usual aim-and-shoot photography. In this age of the 'guerilla' photographer[50] who roams the country shamelessly reducing all to public images, photography is better described as 'an acute manifestation of the individualized "I".'[51] As Sontag observes, these photographers 'reject any ambition to pre-visualize the image and conceive their work as showing how different things look when photographed.'[52] In contrast to the self-effacement of the waist-level photographer, these photographers are voyeuristic. The mechanical gaze creates 'estrangement from, rather than union with, nature.'[53] Guerilla photography is a modern manifestation of man the predator, objectifying the world. 'Despite the illusion of giving understanding, what seeing through photographs really invites is an acquisitive relation to the world that nourishes aesthetic awareness and promotes emotional detachment.'[54]

Sontag is speaking of photography in general, and she might well reject this distinction between the overtly staring photographers of today and the image-gardeners who were more common in the past. But in any event, the profound effect she attributes to photography is certainly consistent with the notion that it is an amplifier of visual dependency and an aid to objectification. But again we must bear in mind that objectification is not a uniquely human phenomenon. Indeed, it might more properly be thought of as a basic animal propensity. Objectification is an inevitable part of the life-rhythm of any being that lives by consuming life. But it is not a permanent condition. It is transitory, something appropriate to only certain situations and something that must routinely be inhibited to prevent erosion of the community. The mood of objectification is necessary for some functions, like predation, but incompatible with others. It is a destructive and isolating state of being. In daily interaction there must be a mood of compliance if there is to be a social unit, and some means of communicating mood between members of the community.

'It' versus 'You'

Earlier in this chapter I have referred to Straus's discussion of shame and his assertion that '"looking at" objectifies.' Apparently his conclusion is not unique, although his thoughts on shame itself may well be. It is significant that the voyeur, the staring man, is constantly invading the sphere of immediate being and thereby transgressing a boundary normally defended by shame. By remaining constantly objective, the voyeur diminishes immediate being and reduces the world to one sphere, the public. The public sphere is objective and repetitive, the immediate singular and based on reciprocity. Those familiar with Martin Buber's description of alternate modes of being may detect some similarity here, at least in intent. Buber contrasts the objective 'I-It' relationship with the reciprocal 'I-Thou' or, as some translators prefer, 'I-You.' Perhaps of all the attempts to describe the human potential for transforming the world Buber's is the most successful. That his book *I and Thou* has been so well received is evidence that it touches something in all of us. It can, at moments at least, fully satisfy us that the reality we occupy depends on the stance we take towards the world, and not on the things we encounter. The 'I' of the two relationships is different in each case. That is, the person is transformed by the kind of relationship established, by the way he or she addresses the other. 'The I of man comes into being in the act of speaking one or the other of these primary words. But the two I's are not the same: "the primary word *I-Thou* can only be spoken with the whole being. The primary word *I-It* can never be spoken with the whole being".'[55]

Perhaps the contrast is best conveyed by an example which Buber uses and which is especially suited to our topic. In contemplating a tree, he says, one can accept it as a picture, a pillar illuminated by colour and shadow; or as a being astir with life, transpiring and growing; or one can classify it according to species and examine its construction; or perhaps even describe it in terms of laws governing the forces of its configuration; or even reduce it to a pure relation of numbers.

Throughout all of this the tree remains my object and has its place and its time span, its kind and condition.

But it can also happen, if will and grace are joined, that as I contemplate the tree I am drawn into a relation, and the tree ceases to be an It. The power of exclusiveness has seized me.

This does not require me to forego any of the modes of contemplation. There is nothing that I must not see in order to see, and there is no knowledge that I must forget. Rather is everything, picture and movement, species and instance, law and number included and inseparably fused.

Whatever belongs to the tree is included: its form and its mechanics, its colors and its chemistry, its conversation with the elements and its conversation with the stars — all this in its entirety.

The tree is no impression, no play of my imagination, no aspect of a mood; it confronts me bodily and has to deal with me as I must deal with it — only differently.

One should not try to dilute the meaning of the relation: relation is reciprocity.

Does the tree then have consciousness, similar to our own? I have no experience of that. But thinking that you have brought this off in your own case, must you again divide the indivisible? What I encounter is neither the soul of the tree nor a dryad, but the tree itself.[56]

One can treat the tree as a thing, or with the tree be part of a reciprocal relationship. The 'I' will be quite different in each instance. It would be unfair simply to equate Buber's insight with all that has been discussed above, but it may improve our understanding if we accept Buber's work as an individual elaboration of a more general insight. All of our discussion in this chapter, and indeed throughout the book, has centred on the relationship of mind to nature, the central concern of human ecology. It is the *kind* of relationship we establish which will determine the world we live in. He who chooses to say 'It' routinely lives in a world of objects. He becomes a professional stranger, the objective observer who, according to Straus, we always feel somewhat threatened by and shamed by. He is the person Tuan speaks of, the watcher who suddenly makes us aware of ourselves as objects in another's gaze. And it is he who, in collaboration with others, sustains a system in which 'a man, a living human being, ceases to be an end in himself, and becomes the means for the economic interests of another man, or himself, or of an impersonal giant, the economic machine.'[57] And it is in such a system that the individual comes to feel himself an automaton, an object among objects. He who says 'It' tries to diminish his own fear of being objectified by removing the source of potential objectification from the world. In denying the subjective existence of everything in nature, he assures himself of safety within his stockade. With relationship denied, there is no reciprocity, and no other to threaten him. Deafness is a requirement, for any hint of subjectivity emanating from the world would be evidence of relatedness. He can avoid

the risk by shunning contact and symbolically cutting the earthly
vocal cords.

When this has been accomplished, he can be sure that the 'correct'
perception of Buber's tree will prevail; trees are material objects and
natural resources. And this view can be bolstered by censorship. To
perceive the tree as anything other than a useful object is to be 'impractical' or 'merely romantic.' It was just such censorship that the
Romantics rebelled against through their refusal to accept any single
'way the world is' and their provocatively ambiguous notion of reality.
Significantly, their conclusions about objectivity and the role of vision
in it bear some similarity to the views outlined above. The Romantics
detected 'a conflict of the faculties, in which the eye was the victor and
assumed the role of tyrant over the subservient mind.'[58] In speaking of
Coleridge's concern with vision M.H. Abrams says that 'of this mastery of the mind by the eye, the results are "selfishness, hate, and
servitude." The beginning of genuine freedom, therefore, is to break
free from the tyrant eye: "to emancipate the mind from the despotism of
the eye".'[59] And Blake, who was especially vehement in his attack on
vision, felt that 'man has lapsed into a fixed and "narrowed" mode of
"single vision" by means of the physical eye alone, which sees reality as
a multitude of isolated individuals in a dehumanized world.'[60] Blake
objected to Locke's analogy of the senses as windows on the world,
and pointed out that it is not the window that sees, but the person within.
When Blake claimed to see through and not with the eye, he implied
that with his human faculties or 'Imagination' he could discern far more
than the mere surfaces of material objects. In his advocacy of higher
modes of perception, of the ability to grasp more than simple physical
presence, he reminds us of more modern writers, like Schumacher
with his plea for the 'adequate' person who is equipped to deal with
more than the lowest common denominator in knowledge. But Blake
also seems to have felt that the objectification that arises from the
reliance on vision is also responsible for the diminishing of man's
sense of worth (his own worth and that of the world). 'Blake held that
man's inhumanity comes about through a morality imposed from
without, whereby we treat our fellow-humans as objects, as other, not as
one in the single life of the living Imagination.'[61] While Blake was not
an apologist for nature as were some of the other Romantics, he did

argue that 'everything that lives is holy.' The implication of such a belief is, according to Kathleen Raine, that it 'must surely become impossible for whoever has seen that there is nothing in creation without life or outside the life of God, to behave towards the created world as does our profane society. We kill without reason or pretext the animals and birds, poison the herbs and the insects, pollute the rivers and the seas, lay waste the earth, cut down the forests, all for material gain or expediency. If we were to see these things in terms of life, could we do these things?'[62]

Could we behave as we do towards the world if we had not this strange unbalanced perception to guide us? This problem must be addressed by anyone who questions the wisdom of modern human enterprise. But whether one thinks in terms of our relation to God, as did Buber and Blake, or in more profane biological terms, the ability of humans effectively to destroy relationship as a possibility through the maintenance of objectivity demands our attention. Indeed, it may be that the stare, the relentless grasp of the stranger on the throat of intimacy, is a virtual prerequisite to modernity. Only the presence of eternal strangers, whom shame cannot restrain, makes possible the unbroken reign of objectivity in which we pride ourselves.

It should be said that there is no intention, either here or in the works cited, to argue that objectivity is in itself an evil to be abolished. Even the most strident of critics would maintain that it is simply one means of perception among many. But none would welcome our near-total reliance on the gaze of objectivity. Indeed, the loss of intimacy and immediacy entailed in our achievement of objectivity could with some justification be cited as the major motivation for the environmental movement throughout its long history. This particular stance denies that which is most basic to the movement: relationship. And in that denial, in the utterance of 'It,' we become persons who are unable to hear the world of life. The world is transformed, and the maps of that world cannot reveal the significant places since, by convention, there are none. But whether we listen or not, the world continues to speak. Display is a basic property of life, and we are a part of its audience. Consciousness cannot construct any dictionary to assist us in discerning what life says when it speaks. The task of understanding is one for each to face alone, without translators. But perhaps we can at least fathom why the language of life seems so remote to us, even as we proclaim ourselves the most advanced beings ever to grace the earth. Perhaps our deafness is congenital.

CHAPTER FIVE

Natural Aliens

Patterns or Pieces

Each organism has its world, and that enables it to function and persist. Each lives within that world to which it is made. The variability of the human world makes it very difficult to speak of humans having *an* environment, for the human surroundings vary with their world. It is this strange flexibility that makes it possible for us to believe in an abstract reality which pits us against, or more correctly separates us from, the earth that houses all organic worlds.

Throughout the discussion so far we have had to pay attention to the official version of the way the world is – also referred to, here as elsewhere, as the Cartesian world-view, the scientistic world-view, or just as the dominant social paradigm – simply because it is this version which determines not only the answers we seem to find but even the questions we can choose to ask. Even to speak of problems and solutions predisposes us to a particular stance in the world, and to particular kinds of understanding. We are at present constrained to a certain set of questions or to a single way the world is. Trying to build a society upon foundations provided by a single kind of knowledge, scientific or otherwise, is certain to result in distortions. Hence E.F. Schumacher's discovery of the deficiency of the maps generated by our society, maps which leave out all those things which are not amenable to quantitative knowing. The parallel between Schumacher and the environmentalist is obvious, in that both are unable to place their concerns on the map provided and so must challenge its adequacy. But Schumacher also addresses himself to objectivity *per se*, and beyond that to the question of wisdom and the search for meaning. In doing so he finds he must question our claims not just to being able to see the truth clearly but to being able to *see* truth at all. Schumacher also associates objectivity with vision, and science with a particular kind of vision:

It was Sir Arthur Eddington (1882–1944) who said: 'Ideally, all our knowledge of the universe could have been reached by visual sensation alone – in fact by the simplest form of visual sensation, colourless and non-stereoscopic.' If this is true (as it well may be), if the scientific picture of the Universe is the result of the use of the sense of sight only, restricted to the use of 'a single, colour-blind eye,' we can hardly expect that picture to show more than an abstract, inhospitable mechanism. The Great Truth of adaequatio *teaches us that restriction in the use of instruments of cognition has the inevitable effect of narrowing and impoverishing reality.*[1]

The benefits of so narrowing our attention are fairly apparent, but the costs may not be: 'We attain objectivity, but we fail to attain knowledge of the *object as a whole*. Only the "lowest," the most superficial, aspects of the object are accessible to the instruments we employ; everything that makes the object humanly interesting, meaningful and significant escapes us.'[2] 'Public knowledge,' that verifiable by anyone with the most rudimentary of perceptual skills, is all that is counted as knowledge, and reality is defined as that which exists in the public sphere rather than in immediate experience.

But Schumacher is confident that we possess the means to perceive much more than this lowest common denominator, and that what is most important can only be perceived by transcending this elementary level. The catch is that the individual must become *capable* of perceiving more, just as the athlete becomes capable of greater physical accomplishments than he could before he prepared himself. It is the acquisition of these refined perceptual skills that is of special interest to Schumacher, who claims that 'we cannot experience any part or facet of the world unless we possess and use an organ or instrument through which we are able to receive what is being offered. If we do not have the requisite organ or instrument, or fail to use it, we are not *adequate* to this particular part or facet of the world, with the result that, as far as we are concerned, it simply does not exist.'[3]

The consequences of this inadequacy are enormous, for it 'follows from this truth that any systematic neglect or restriction in the use of our organs of cognition must inevitably have the effect of making the world appear less meaningful, rich, interesting, and so on than it actually is.'[4] So long as we neglect the development of perceptual skills, the world is diminished in equal measure. As our awareness expands, so too does the reality we inhabit. The challenge is to prevent further diminution of the world we dwell in by reversing the trend to lower levels of apprehension. But how is this to be accomplished, particularly since it is the belief of our society that we currently stand at the pinnacle of understanding? Of course, the point is that we excel at only one kind of knowledge and ignore others of greater significance to the individual. And indeed, although this is not Schumacher's claim, it may be that non-human beings have easier access to some of these other insights than do we. But for now the main point is simply that there is more than one kind of knowledge, and that the one we choose to emphasize may pale in significance beside those we ignore.

Consider the thesis of Alfred North Whitehead, as expressed in his book *Symbolism, Its Meaning and Effect*. In this small volume, published in 1927 (about the same time as Husserl was publishing his early work), Whitehead identified two different modes of perception which he termed 'presentational immediacy' and 'causal efficacy.' These terms have a philosophic significance and were appropriate to the context in which he was writing, but they are rather awkward for our purposes. Colin Wilson has suggested as alternatives 'immediacy-perception' and 'meaning-perception,'[5] but I think we may simplify even further by calling them 'detail-perception' and 'meaning-perception' (with the proviso that the new terms naturally obscure the meaning of the original to some degree, and with the recommendation that the interested reader turn to the original for a richer description). Detail-perception is what we think of as normal sensation – the reception of the various environmental stimuli. It provides us with an array of simple empirical facts. But meaning-perception involves the detection of wholes. We may say that instead of the perception of words, we are concerned with the meaning of the sentence. Whitehead describes his detail-perception (presentational immediacy) as 'our immediate perception of the contemporary external world, appearing as an element constitutive of our own experience. In this appearance the world discloses itself to be a community of actual things, which are actual in the same sense we are.'[6] But he adds that 'the disclosure of a contemporary world by presentational immediacy is bound up with the disclosure of the solidarity of actual things by reason of their participation in an impartial system of spatial extension. Beyond this, the knowledge provided by pure presentational immediacy is vivid, precise, and barren.'[7] The world disclosed by this accumulation of fact is 'intrinsically meaningless.' It shows us the pieces, but never the connections, and certainly not the meanings.

Meaning-perception is the broader and the less precise of the two kinds of perception, but it gives us the sense of connectedness and consistency we find in life. And while we may be inclined to assume that the simple reception of sensory facts is the most basic and primitive kind of knowledge, Whitehead concludes that meaning-perception is actually more basic. Instead of simple details, barren and meaningless in themselves, meaning-perception provides a primitive, intuitive understanding of the rightness of events. By this the organism is able to detect not objects but context, the meaning of its world. It provides the organism with what it must know.

In applying Whitehead's distinction to a description of contemporary humanity Wilson concludes that our misguided fondness of detail-perception has led us seriously astray. Detail-perception, which presents us with clearcut objects, provides exactly what Descartes required as the raw material for his new science. Subsequently there has been a tendency to ignore the alternate mode and to attempt to build a whole from just one source. According to Wilson:

Man is in the position of a painter painting a gigantic canvas. If he is close enough to be able to work, he is too close to see it as a whole. If he stands back to see it as a whole, he is too far away to use his paint-brush. The natural solution for the painter would be to move back and forth as often as possible. But the scientist would feel that such conduct was unscientific. He keeps his nose to the canvas, and creates 'theories' to unify his facts. Science begins with the facts, proceeds to theory, then returns to the facts to verify or disprove the theory. The scientist has no use for meaning-perception – at least in theory. In fact, any good scientist or mathematician will admit that imagination is as indispensable to the scientist as to the poet; still, one will find no mention of this in books on scientific method.[8]

Wilson continues his analogy, pointing out that an art critic who paid attention only to the texture of the paint would miss the whole point of the picture. And, of course, the implication is that this is what we in western culture habitually do: study the details and miss the point, and then make up a theory to substitute for the point that is missed. It was suggested earlier that science could be regarded as a series of tested guesses, and that the most curious feature of our daily existence is that we now accept 'facts' (science-derived guesses) in preference to our own experiences or perceptions of meaning. Wilson is suggesting that whatever our preferences and however much we may admire the evidence of detail-perception, it is through meaning-perception that we live. Indeed Whitehead, in describing causal efficacy as the most basic of the two modes of perception, implies that so-called lower creatures are able to function with this mode alone. This is a puzzling suggestion at first, since we normally assume that any creature must receive the raw facts of its environment, even though its low intelligence may limit what it can make of the evidence. In contrast, Whitehead says that such creatures must know what makes sense, not what simply exists 'out there.' Even though we have heightened ability to discriminate such factual evidence about our surroundings, we too have a basic reliance on meaning-perception to provide the context of our actions. We must be able to see the whole painting, however adept we may be at examining brush-strokes. Meaning-perception (causal efficacy) 'is the experience dominating the primitive living organisms, which have a sense for the fate from which they have emerged, and for the fate toward which they go.'[9]

It becomes increasingly apparent that there are many different ways of approaching the world, and that what we call 'objectivity' is but one of them. It is not an absolute, not the epitome of consciousness, but a stance in the world. Neither is it unique to humans, although the extent of its use certainly is. But perhaps all this is more understandable in the light of Whitehead's description of these contrasting but complementary modes of perception. If it is a matter of balancing the relative influence accorded each of these modes, then contemporary human consciousness becomes more understandable, both in its successes and its failures. Perhaps the most interesting feature of all is the very flexibility it implies, the ability of a creature actually to become a different kind of being through a shift in its style of perception. Yet it may be that, even if the flexibility itself is a human feat, the consequence of eclipsing the means of grasping context and meaning is shared by at least a few of our fellow creatures. Those organisms which we term 'exotics' – creatures living outside their native environment – may share our sense of aimlessness despite the 'success' their fecundity affords.

Exotics

In 1958 Charles Elton published *The Ecology of Invasions by Animals and Plants,* in which he describes the strange behaviour that often accompanies a shift to an environment in which the organism did not evolve. Often it will promptly disappear, but occasionally such an organism will flourish and 'explode' in numbers. This is often explained by the absence of natural predators in the new environment to constrain it, despite the fact that it is doubtful whether predators are ever a significant factor in the depletion of animal numbers, at least in higher vertebrates. For example, the lion is the only major predator of the wildebeest of the Serengeti Plains, but the 12,000 to 18,000 animals lions take from the herd of 200,000 annually are too few to affect the herd. In fact, a far greater cause of mortality is calves getting lost in the herd and being unable to find their mothers.[10] Yet so firmly entrenched is our belief in the voracious appetites of predators that a decline in population size is assumed to be caused by predators and an increase by their absence. In the case of exotics, it is doubtful that release from predation can account for the increase, except perhaps in the case of invertebrates.

In some instances it is believed that the exotic animal encounters an empty niche, a means of living which is not being used by anything else. In such cases, for example, starlings in North American cities, the results are spectacular. But often the explosion in numbers is not easily explained away. Why have these species not become equally abundant

in their native habitat? What has happened to effect this change in
reproductive behaviour or density tolerance? It is in the nature of our
understanding of reality to look for an external mode of control, for the
notion of self-regulation strikes us as improbable (hence belief of the
Roman Catholic Church that birth control is unnatural despite the fact
that it is a natural feature of most vertebrate populations). We are
expert in 'external' thinking and action. And we too are exotics.

That is to say, we too exist in environments which we did not evolve,
and we too grow unchecked until food becomes a limiting factor –
something very rare among vertebrates. But surely there must be a
natural habitat for humans too? Somewhere – Africa, perhaps – we
must have lived a life 'in harmony' with the biotic community, must we
not? Perhaps. But, paradoxically, we are an exotic organism even in our
place of origin, wherever that might be.[11] We are exotic in any environment, for in a sense we did not evolve *in* any existing habitat. I say 'in a
sense,' for of course we were a part of local ecosystems during most of
our history. But in our minds we may have fallen out of context a very
long time ago, or at least begun so to fall. With the development of
tools our situation changed rather abruptly. A tool may be thought of as
an extension of the individual who uses it. Such an extension effectively constitutes the transformation of the individual into a new kind of
being. A person with a tool is capable of a kind of behaviour which
was formerly difficult or impossible. A man who invents a spear instantly
becomes a new and more dangerous kind of predator. Both his life
and that of his new prey are radically transformed. The consequences of
technology are subtle but extensive, and one such consequence is that
humans cannot evolve *with* an ecosystem anywhere. With every technological change we instantly mutate into a new – and for the ecosystem an
exotic – kind of creature. Like other exotics, we are a paradox, a problem for both our environment and ourselves. We search for explanations in terms of external controls or worldly problems, but it may be
more profitable to concentrate on our own confusion. For it is not just
the biotic community that is puzzled by the arrival of the exotic; so too is
the creature itself. Figuratively speaking, just as the environment does
not know how to cope with the new creature, neither does the exotic
know what it ought to do. In other words, the exotic is a problem
because it does not know how to comply. It has no sense of context, no

relatedness to the community of which it is a part. The creature is suspended in ignorance, capable of material existence but not of community commitment.

To speak of commitment to an organic community makes no sense in a world in which there are just 'two things,' as one resource manager said, 'humans and natural resources.'[12] But perhaps it will, as the discussion unfolds. Whitehead gives us a starting-point by recognizing a means of perceiving a context, and John Livingston has offered the term 'compliance' as a description of behaviour he has observed in his vast experience as a naturalist.[13] For the moment I must ask the reader to accept the suggestion that there is a tendency among organisms, or at least social organisms, to behave in such a way as to comply with the imperatives which favour the success of the group as a whole, and possibly the community as a whole. In the example cited above, technological innovation creates a new kind of predator which can compete with the organically evolved specialists. But this throws the technologically altered being out of register with its own community and its own place. Imagine yourself waking up tomorrow as a lion, or a heron. You may be able to kill antelope or spear fish, but will you have any sense of the subtleties of your new existence? Will you understand how to behave, or why? Will you have a sense of identity at all? Or will you be painfully confused about what you ought to do, forced to set about devising mythologies to instruct yourself and your confrères about how to behave and what destiny to seek? Technology displaces its creator and sets him adrift in a world suddenly devoid of sense.

We find ourselves unable to comply for we are ignorant of how to do so, or even of who we are. Like Alice in Wonderland, we are trying to play a game with other beings who do not know our newly invented rules, or we their ancient ones. Gregory Bateson uses the example of Alice playing croquet with the flamingo mallet and the hedgehog ball to illustrate the problems caused by 'the inappropriate coupling of biological systems.'

Alice's difficulty arises from the fact that she does not 'understand' the flamingo, i.e., she does not have systemic information about the 'system' which confronts her. Similarly, the flamingo does not understand Alice. They are at 'cross-purposes.' The problem of coupling man through consciousness with his biological environment is comparable. If consciousness lacks information about the nature of man and the environment, or if the information is distorted and inappropriately selected, then the coupling is likely to generate meta-random sequence of events.[14]

To generate a set of random events is to create a world that does not make sense. Alice is an exotic in Wonderland, with no idea at all of how she should behave, or what it all means. We, like Alice, continue to search for the magic elixirs that will allow us to squeeze back into a world we would know as home. Not only do we lack knowledge of how and for whom to care, but part of our new technological being hinges on the ability *not* to care, to remain dispassionate, unattached, and objective. This enables us to emphasize a kind of world, achieved through one mode of perception. But we also obscure that which is most important to us as living creatures. We gain explicit, barren fact and a world populated with useful things, but we lose all memory of why we are doing this at all, or why we *are*.

Culture, Biology, Neoteny

I have referred earlier to the work of Adolph Portmann, a biologist who confronts aspects of life that are usually ignored or even denied by mainstream biology. He claims, for example, that such phenomena as territoriality have helped draw attention to the significance of the subject, for without the subject there simply is no territory. It is not something we can discover in the world independent of the lives that enact it. It must be revealed to us by a living being as the evidence of that being's inwardness. We have also noted earlier Marjorie Grene's suggestion that Portmann's 'frank avowal of existence of the subject' may have far-reaching consequences for biological research, if others follow his lead. This is especially relevant to what follows, but first we must consider another of Portmann's observations, one which speaks directly to the behavioural flexibility that humans so obviously exhibit.

Portmann asserts that humans are, in effect, organisms without a niche. We are creatures without a predetermined role, who must create ourselves anew in each generation and in the process undergo what we call 'cultural evolution.' These are claims that have been made by a variety of writers, but Portmann is unique in two respects. First, he is not convinced that the concepts of micromutation and selection are sufficient in themselves to explain evolutionary phenomena. But second, and more important in this context, his comparative studies of vertebrate development, and particularly postembryonic development, have led him to a particular understanding of humans. He emphasizes the biological basis of our cultural dexterity and enables us to see ourselves both as participants in the natural world and as humans in a social world.

Portmann explains what he means through reference to two common patterns in vertebrate development. Those which produce young that are relatively immature at birth and must develop for fairly long periods in the nest are referred to as 'nidicolous' species. In contrast, the 'nidifugous' species produce young that are free-moving from the start and need not spend time in the nest. Their eyes are open and they are aware of the world from the outset. In mammals this latter pattern is considered the more advanced. More primitive species produce a large number of nest-bound young (many of which perish), while the advanced forms produce a few alert young. But humans do not fit easily into either category. We are born with our eyes open and in small numbers, but we are also born to a long period of nest-dependence. We are best described as 'secondarily nidicolous.' We have a post-birth gestation, a social gestation, that other mammals do not require. 'In short,' says Grene, 'the whole biological development of a typical mammal has been rewritten in our case in a new key: the whole structure of the embryo, the whole rhythm of growth, is directed, from first to last, to the emergence of a culture-dwelling animal – an animal not bound within a predetermined ecological niche like the tern or the stag or the dragonfly or even the chimpanzee, but, in its very tissues and organs and aptitudes, born to be *open to its world*, to be able to accept responsibility, to make its own the traditions of a historical past and to remake them into an unforeseeable future.'[15]

In general tone this view of man seems consistent with the existentialists' account of man as a species for which 'existence precedes essence' and in which each individual is what he becomes. However, Portmann has embedded his observations in a biological matrix, so as to make it an understandable phenomenon in the world of nature. Humanity is, so to speak, biologically destined to be nicheless.

Yet there are hints in Portmann of a slightly different understanding of humanity as a biological phenomenon. It may be that they are hints he would rather we ignored, since they lead to a kind of explanation which he may regard as premature or even unnecessary, and about which he has particular reservations.[16] Nevertheless, the parallels are so tempting that they cannot be altogether ignored. Bearing in mind that it is this essential openness that is of particular concern, let us see if it is in any way illuminated by the following possibility.

In some instances an intelligent observation may be all that is needed to facilitate a new line of thought. Newton observed that bodies attract, and although he was criticized for not describing the mechanism of this attraction, he was able to use that observation to help explain the astronomical problems before him. Gravity helped make sense of the world and was adopted relatively quickly. In contrast, Darwin and his predecessors had an additional problem. Their observation – that the forms of life change over time – was not particularly difficult or uncommon, but it ran sufficiently contrary to societal expectations and desires that it could not be accepted as an observation. Like Newton, Darwin's predecessors were challenged to show how such a thing could be – what the mechanism of its operation was – but, unlike him, they could not escape that challenge. It was Darwin's great accomplishment to be the first to propose a plausible mechanism. His famous theory was not 'evolution,' as is commonly thought, but the mechanism *of* evolution, which he called 'natural selection.' And the chief benefit of this theory was not so much that it explained how evolution could occur as that it made the observation acceptable to a wider range of society. Newton could use gravity to help understand the world without explaining how it works. Biologists could use evolution to help understand the world of life only after Darwin had shown how it *might* work. But there was never any reason to presume that Darwin's mechanism was the only one possible, or even that it is the only one operating. And, indeed, there have been many modifications and alternatives proposed, which are often construed by anti-evolutionists as rejections of the theory of evolution rather than as what they are, refined explanations for the observation of evolution. And it is one of these refinements that is suggested by Portmann's work.

While Darwin's theory suggests how change can occur through gradual accumulation over time, it does not address the problem of how one population of organisms can become absolutely distinct from its near relatives – in other words, how separate species come into existence. Neither does it explain instances of rapid evolution, since natural selection is presumed to be a slow and gradual process. Naturally, alternative explanations were sought to explain the sudden separation of a line of life into differing species. And one phenomenon has been observed which seems to account for such a change. It is known that in certain organisms the separation is brought about by a change in the rate of development among some individuals. More precisely, development is slowed so dramatically that the individuals never achieve adult form. They remain juvenile in form even when they are chronologically adult, but equally important, they do mature in one important regard: they are able to reproduce. The retention of juvenile form is called 'paedomorphosis,' and the ability to breed while in juvenile form is called 'neoteny.' However, it is common to use the term 'neoteny' to refer to the entire phenomenon. And neoteny is sometimes referred to as a means of speciation. That is, it is one way in which one species can quite abruptly become two. It may be misleading to refer to this as a mechanism of evolution, since we still do not know what brings about the change in rate of development, but at least it is an observation of one kind of change. And it has been suggested (not by Portmann, I must stress) that it is an avenue of evolution that fits rather well with what we know of human development.

It has long been apparent that we have much in common with other primates. But what is more important is that we have a lot more in common with primate infants than with primate adults. Arthur Koestler has summarized the evidence thus:

It is now generally recognised that the human adult resembles more the embryo of an ape than an adult ape. In both simian embryo and human adult, the ratio of the weight of the brain to total body weight is disproportionately high. In both, the closing of the sutures between the bones of the skull is retarded to permit the brain to expand. The back-to-front axis through man's head – i.e., the direction of his line of sight – is at right angles to his spinal column: a condition which, in apes and other mammals, is found only in the embryonic, not in the adult stage.[17]

These, in addition to the more obvious similarities (hairlessness, absence

of brow ridges, lightness of skin, diminished tooth growth), make
plausible the suggestion that human evolution from a proto-human
ancestor could have occurred quite abruptly through paedomorphosis. (Koestler reminds us of a novel by Aldous Huxley in which a
man who has managed to prolong his life artificially far beyond the
normal span learns to his horror that the consequence is his development to the ape-like adult form normally concealed by our retarded
development). Koestler suggests that such a tactic may give a species the
opportunity to escape its mistakes and draw back to take a new
initiative. But what exactly does a species divest itself of when it follows
this course of development? There is no suggestion that only the
undesirable attributes of the adult are lost. The entire creature is set
back to some more general level, and much of what was explicit in the
final form is no longer in evidence. But while we can see well enough
what has been lost in morphological development by comparing a
paedomorphic form with its ancestral pattern, we cannot examine any
fossilized 'behaviours.' In other words, we may see the changes in
gross form that have occurred, but we cannot detect alterations in the
overall pattern of functioning. Yet if there are significant changes in
morphology, it does not seem presumptuous to expect that there may
also be changes in functioning, including behaviour. Even allowing
for the controversial status of innate behaviour in humans, it may not be
out of line to ask whether, since the physical rates of human development are apparently unique and consistent with the hypothesis of neotenic development, it is not plausible that some behavioural tendencies
may have changed as well.

Indeed, is this not the very thing of which we are so proud, our
delayed development with its potential for increased learning? I am not
suggesting a change in the kinds of innate behaviour humans exhibit,
but a regression from the overt expression of such behaviour at all. This
may be one of the things that does not develop to the more concrete and
inflexible form common to more 'finished' animals. In short, if we are
what we are partly through the retention of juvenile form, might that
not also imply the retention of certain juvenile predispositions in
thought and behaviour as well? Perhaps that can only be answered by
addressing another question, namely 'what are the characteristics of
youthfulness?'

Youth and Openness

To answer this question, we must turn to another of the unusual biologists discussed by Grene in her *Approaches to a Philosophical Biology*. F.J.J. Buytendijk uses the methods of phenomenology to try to describe certain of the properties of life, among them 'youthfulness' in vertebrates. He identifies four such properties, the first of which is 'want of direction.' As Grene translates it, 'youthful activity springs from an indeterminate cause and moves in no particular direction ... There is a lack of direct adaptation to the environment, yet not the kind of nonadaptation that marks stupidity.'[18] There are no obvious goals for youthful creatures, and therefore no sense of wilful direction towards them. 'Indeterminate' may be the best single adjective for such an individual.

Second, there is the 'drive to movement,' something which it would be hard for any observer to avoid noticing. The young animal is never passive, but 'acts first on the environment.' 'The conjunction of undirectedness and the drive to movement produces an instability which is only later to be replaced by fixed reactions.'[19] An image begins to emerge of a being which is eager, even driven, and yet unaware of any purpose in its motion. It must search but never find.

The third property, more difficult to describe, concerns the 'characteristically pathic' behaviour of youth. This refers to a distinction made by Erwin Straus between what he calls 'pathic' and 'gnostic' behaviour. The gnostic is the 'primitive forerunner of the cognitive,' while the pathic is 'the immediate communication we have with things on the basis of their changing mode of sensory givenness.'[20] The pathic is more immediate and may seem to us a more naïve form of knowing. 'The pathic is directed to the *how*: the immediate tones, feelings, appearances of environmental happenings as they meet the organism in its dawning awareness ... It is not inexperience, but nondirectedness, that produces the pathic mode of being: "youth does not yet live with the environment, is not yet directed to it." '[21] Since it concerns the relationship with environment, this property may be especially significant to our discussion.

The fourth property that Buytendijk identifies is shyness, 'an ambiguity of the to and fro.' This hovering between the home and the outside, between family membership and individuality, is not at all like fear but is an ambivalence that fades with age and its consequent sense of certainty or purpose. 'When the new, developed relation between organism and environment has been established, shyness disappears.'[22] Significantly, shyness is not found in nidifugous species, in which there is no ambiguity about the relationship to environment even at birth.

We might summarize all these as a description of a placeless creature, an organism indeterminate in its being and unrelated to its environment. It is an undecided, uncommitted creature awaiting resolution. In Buytendijk's own words:

> The youthful being appears to us as one that is open in a special way, not in the sense of an intentional openness, but rather as an indeterminate receptivity, not yet hardened and not yet directed. To be youthful is to be not yet fitted into situations, to be not yet the complement of a projected world and a projected action. This is an important point. It reveals the grace of youthfulness, but reveals also the very well-founded thought that that which is most essential to the human being is precisely the human's transcendence over nature. The animal stature is suited only to its own special world, as the key is suited to the lock. Man on the other hand is everywhere at home, or nowhere.[23]

We must remember that Buytendijk is describing youthfulness as a property of vertebrates, not just of humans. And he also speaks of maturity in all vertebrates. But in this statement he is apparently allowing that youthfulness is a property of humanity in general, and not just of juveniles. And his descriptions seem to fit quite well with Portmann's characterization of humanity as a 'nicheless' creature at home everywhere or nowhere. Furthermore, the qualities described are just those we might expect of an organism which retains in some measure its immature form. That is, if the conjecture of neotenic development in humans is correct, then it is not at all surprising that the qualities which describe youthfulness in other species also apply to a creature which owes its very form to a slowed or arrested development. We are just what a perpetually youthful being should be: indeterminate, always in motion, ambivalent, obsessed with the 'how' of the world, and uncommitted to an environmental context.

What all this would mean is that the human orientation towards the world makes perfect biological sense. Nor should we regard this as an implausible or freakish occurrence – neoteny and paedomorphosis may not be unusual means of development in the organic world. They are significant devices for jumping out of an evolutionary rut. The conclusions of Portmann and the many others who have speculated on the indeterminate properties of humanity are entirely consistent with this possibility, even though some of these biologists might feel uncomfortable about associating human development with normal evolutionary processes. But this convergence does cast a different light on our situation. Consider the existentialist, for example, who would argue that there is no such thing as human nature, and that for humans existence precedes essence. In one sense, the pattern of development outlined above would tend to corroborate his beliefs. Yes, man is born without a plan, but he seems nicheless, not because he has gone beyond such pedestrian developments, but because he has backed away from them. By retaining an immature form throughout man never realizes his final one, and so he escapes (or is deprived of) definition. Unfortunately, this admission tends to obscure the fact that man is still a biological being. A person falling off a cliff may be said to have freedom of choice in whether to fall feet first or to attempt a swan dive, but no choice of position will negate the central fact of his fall. Man remains in nature even if the range of choice he enjoys seems incomparably greater than that of other species. Others are made to their world, while man must construct one with constant risk of error.

There is an important distinction to be made between the descriptions of humanity made by the existentialists and those made by the biologists. To the former man's freedom is an accomplishment, however terrible or wonderful its consequences. Man has transcended nature. He is freed of it, he makes himself. The biologist agrees that man must make himself in some degree, but not because he has transcended nature. Rather, it is because his rate of development is so altered that he no longer reaches a final resolution as a creature explicitly fitted to an environment. The difference in the two positions is one of bias. The existentialist's is totally anthropocentric, often openly contemptuous of nature. He is offended by the placement of man in nature, or by the slightest hint of determinacy or predisposition. He rejoices in man's escape from nature. But to the biologist this escape is at most an admission of the obvious. Indeed, Mary Midgley has argued that 'the really monstrous thing about Existentialism too is its proceeding as if the world contained only dead matter (things) on the one hand and fully rational, educated, adult human beings on the other – as if there were no other life-forms. The impression of *desertion* or *abandonment* which Existentialists have is due, I am sure, not to the removal of God, but to this contemptuous dismissal of almost the whole biosphere – plants, animals, and children.'[24] I mention this, not to discredit existentialism, which has a valuable contribution to make to the issue in question, but to point out the contradiction some may see in using the work of phenomenologists in a discussion of environmentalism. Since there has been a prominent connection between phenomenology and existentialism, it is well to remember that the two are not identical. The biologists referred to in this chapter amply demonstrate that the realization of human flexibility need not lead to a dismissal of all of creation. The use of phenomenology need not lead to Sartre but can lead instead to the more environmentally positive insights of Merleau-Ponty, Heidegger, or Portmann.

Indeed, as we have seen through the example of Heidegger, the realization of human homelessness need not lead to the despair so often associated with existentialism. And if we pause to recall a few of Heidegger's conclusions, we may find some measure of congruence with those of the biologists cited above, even though Heidegger would probably be apprehensive about this and eager to avoid 'biologisms.'

Heidegger speaks to 'the essential homelessness of man' and describes characteristics that seem, in retrospect, strikingly familiar. For example, he speaks of 'idle talk' which 'discloses to *Dasein* a Being towards its world, towards Others and towards itself – a Being in which these are understood, but in a mode of groundless floating.' Also, he says that ambiguity 'hides nothing from *Dasein*'s understanding, but only in order that Being-in-the-world should be suppressed in this uprooted "everywhere and nowhere".'[25] And perhaps most interesting is what he says of curiosity:

Curiosity has nothing to do with observing entities and marvelling at them ... To be amazed to the point of not understanding is something in which it has no interest. Rather it concerns itself with a kind of knowing, but just in order to have known. Both this not tarrying in the environment with which one concerns oneself, and this distraction by new possibilities, are constitutive items for curiosity; and upon these is founded the third essential characteristic of this phenomenon, which we call the character of 'never dwelling anywhere' ... *This mode of Being-in-the-world reveals a new kind of Being of everyday Dasein – a kind in which Dasein is constantly uprooting itself.*[26]

This picture of 'groundless floating,' of being 'everywhere and nowhere' and of 'never dwelling anywhere,' seems essentially similar to Buytendijk's description of the youthful being who is 'not yet fitted into situations' and who is 'everywhere at home, or nowhere.' Both are descriptions of placeless beings. However, there is no implication in Heidegger that this is an inevitable condition, only that it is one of the possibilities open to humans. It does seem to be one we are strongly disposed to, and this disposition is something Heidegger speaks to. The statements cited above pertain to the possibility of falling into a particular manner of existence, but the alternative to this may give us grounds for hope.

Heidegger characterizes us as beings for whom Being is an issue, and related to that awareness is a particular mood of anxiety. We may say that this anxiety is the consequence of our ability to see our own medium, to be aware of Being. That medium is perceptible because we have withdrawn from it to a degree. And that withdrawal, which leaves us out of place and lacking the comforting embrace of home that is the daily condition of our earthly companions, enables us, like travellers in a foreign land, to perceive that which is taken for granted by placeful beings. This situation of being 'held in abeyance' leaves us open to the existence of possibilities. But not only is it the case that 'anxiety discloses Dasein *as being-possible*';[27] Heidegger also claims that 'in anxiety one feels *"uncanny"* and that here *"uncanniness"* also means *"not-being at-home"*.'[28] In anxiety the world falls away and loses all significance, so that one is unattached, at home nowhere.

But in the face of anxiety one may respond in different ways. One may retreat from the awful realization or embrace it. If we choose to repress it, then we fall into a different mode of Being. We seek an ersatz place: 'When in falling we flee *into* the "at-home" of publicness, we flee *in the face of* the "not-at-home"; that is, we flee in the face of the uncanniness which lies in Dasein.'[29] The publicness that is turned to is the 'they,' the collective reassurance of participation in mass society. By being one of the crowd and immersing ourselves in the trivia of mass existence we attempt to conceal our placelessness from ourselves. In effect, we establish, through common consensus, a make-believe place to point to when the 'sacred horror' confronts us in the night. This is a perfectly genuine option for us, not just a modern anomaly. To phrase it in a way consistent with our earlier discussion, we may act as if we were finished beings by inventing a place for ourselves. But the deceit works only with the complicity of the group, which must act as if 'that's all there is' – as if there were no edges to the plateau we inhabit and therefore no danger of slipping off into the abyss. Without that co-operative illusion we are left to confront our situation squarely, and to discover that we need not choose to sustain ourselves in perpetual youthfulness and collective forgetfulness.

Heidegger, of course, does not discuss it in these terms. To do so might be incompatible with his project. But the parallels drawn above between his insights and those of others may serve to cast a different light on both. The analogy may be drawn between the alternatives open to us. Heidegger speaks of the possibility of achieving an authentic existence that would let us accept our role as the neighbours of Being. The analogous possibility might be the attaining of some semblance of maturity through the process of social gestation. Portmann concludes:

We can thus say that the growing human being is born out of the mother's body into a second uterus in which he traverses the second half of his embryonic life: this is the social *uterus. Thereby we also characterize the mighty task of society; we see more clearly how much the success or failure of the individual life depends on this decisive early epoch.*[30]

Our failures in this social gestation have been dramatically revealed by Paul Shepard.[31] But for our purposes what is significant is the possibility that remains. No matter that the options chosen seem to foreclose so much, and to confine us within a funnel of our own making that leads to inauthenticity and perhaps to annihilation; there always remains another way, and the possibility of a human homecoming. The portrait of humanity drawn by Portmann and Buytendijk is one of an inevitably youthful being condemned to ambivalence and place-lessness. But these are companions to its essential *openness*, and the social gestation admits of the possibility of a different resolution. We may well be predisposed to act as universal exotics, but it would be pointless to conclude that that is all we are or may become.

Natural Aliens

To draw together the diverse threads of this chapter, I must suggest that if something like meaning-perception or context-sensitivity can be regarded as being of fundamental biological significance, then we have cause to wonder whenever some organism displays environmental intemperance. The phenomenon of the exotic organism is one that seems indicative of a systemic 'misunderstanding': the organism seems unable to make sense of its place in the community it finds itself in. I have suggested that there are grounds for regarding humans as exotics of a sort, since technological innovation may effectively cast its creator out of context. But it may be that the source of human indeterminism and ambiguity is more fundamental than that of an environmental misfit. Perhaps the very mode of development of our species is such as to inhibit refinement of the perceptual abilities which could facilitate our occupancy of a particular place in the organic world. Hence, our situation may be only superficially similar to that of other exotics, since even though we share their confusion over a context with which we have inadequate evolutionary experience, we may also lack full use of the abilities which give our more placeful contem-poraries 'a sense of the fate from which they have emerged, and for the fate toward which they go.' As perennially youthful creatures, ambival-ent, agitated, and uncommitted to an environment, we inevitably lack that sense of direction and purpose implicit to the notion of *Umwelt*. By organic standards this is a monumental deformity. Coleridge fre-quently lamented the tendency to divide – nature from mind, subject from object, thing from thought, and so forth – and the philosophy that encourages it. 'To the materialists, accordingly, nature is "the natu-ral alien of their negative eye," and the mechanical philosophy, in separating off phenomena from the living mind, "strikes death through all things visible and invisible".'[32] But in the sense used here, it is we who are the natural aliens.

This need not be an entirely pessimistic conclusion, since the same deformity which sets us apart from that place that was essentially our own definition also constitutes the source of an amazing, if dangerous, flexibility. Through our secondary social gestation a panorama of options is revealed, alternative mythologies that characterize the various cultures. The need for culture derives from an underlying, biologically given state of suspension, but the promise of culture is apparent to the most cynical – if, that is, it is not so personally distorting as to result in a collection of pathological selves with little potential for the constituting of reciprocal relationships.[33] There is certainly nothing new in the notion that human beings stand apart from nature. But I suspect that the understanding of humans as creatures who have withdrawn from finished animality and are now condemned to work out a secondary maturation process does give us a slightly different understanding of ourselves and our consequences. As premature beings we are reliant on a kind of incubator for survival, but the incubator serves, not to sustain metabolism until the body can survive autonomously, but to sustain belief so that the individual can survive psychically. Culture is, so to speak, the glass in which we see darkly that which has been discarded.

There is no hope of untangling the biological and the cultural in the amalgam that is human. We are given to culture by virtue of our situation in the organic world, and culture remains our sole apparent means of approximating the meaning which habitually evades us. That approximation may be of far greater significance than we commonly admit. Indeed, Viktor Frankl developed his own highly successful mode of psychiatric treatment on just this insight: those who endure are those for whom life has significance. I have merely been suggesting that this is inevitable: a cultural search for meaning, if successful, may alleviate the symptoms of placelessness to which we are biologically disposed. But, of course, the cultural amelioration is not always successful, and when it is not, symptoms of exoticism stand forth. When the story fails, when it no longer satisfies, the anxiety of individuals will be revealed again. Environmentalism is one such revelation of anxiety and concern over the failure of the cultural explanation. In denuding the world of significance the modern version of reality generates apprehension and perhaps false bravado as well. As Hans Jonas argues, the 'waiving of the intelligibility of life – the price which modern knowledge was willing to pay for its title to the greater part of reality – renders the world unintelligible as well.'[34] This particular cultural guess does not satisfy the requirement of giving meaning to existence. In fact, such a world-view is very nearly the antithesis of the curative that environmentalists seek. For although they seldom recognize it, they are protesting not the stripping of natural resources but the stripping of earthly meaning. I have suggested earlier that environmentalism, like Romanticism, constitutes a defence of value. I am now asserting an even more fundamental role, the defence of meaning. We call people environmentalists because what they are finally moved to defend is what we call environment. But, at bottom, their action is a defence of cosmos, not scenery. Ironically, the very entity they defend – environment – is itself an offspring of the nihilistic behemoth they challenge. It is a manifestation of the way we view the world.

CHAPTER SIX

The Shells of Belief

Environment and Belief

The term 'environmentalist' was not chosen by the individuals so
described. It was seized upon by members of the popular press as a
means of labelling a newly prominent segment of society. But, of
course, any term selected by the news media is likely to be drawn from
common usage and to reflect common assumptions. It is difficult to
imagine, therefore, that this agent would have great success in concisely
describing something distinctly *un*common. In fact, the act of labelling a group may constitute an effective means of suppression, even if
the label seems neutral or objective. For in giving this particular
name, not only have the labellers forced an artificial association on a very
diverse group of individuals, but they have also given a terse public
statement of what 'those people' are presumed to want. Environmentalists want environment – obviously. But this may be entirely wrong, a
possibility that few environmentalists have contemplated even though
many have lamented the term itself. For in a very real sense there can
only *be* environment in a society that holds certain assumptions, and
there can only be an environmental crisis in a society that believes in
environment.

Just what an environment is may not be as evident as we assume.
Mary Douglas's reminder that any environment we know 'exists as a
structure of meaningful distinctions'[1] should dissuade us of the notion
that environments are disconnected from social belief. But in standard

usage we do treat environment as a simply physical entity. The *Concise Oxford Dictionary* defines it as 'surrounding; surrounding objects, region, or circumstances.' But such a definition may only be possible in our times, for it is only since the Renaissance that there has been an abundance of identifiable objects with which to surround ourselves. Of course, there have always been 'things,' but, as Oscar Wilde claimed, no one saw the mists on the Thames until artists had painted them. The environment exists because it was made visible by the act of making it separate. It exists because we have excised it from the context of our lives. J.H. van den Berg has suggested that a particular transformation is indicated by Leonardo's *Mona Lisa*. Two things, he claims, are revealed in that painting: the emergence of the individual, and the emergence of landscape. Again, there were certainly landscapes and figures in paintings before Leonardo, just as there were mists on the Thames before Turner and things before Descartes. But after these tutors have shown us the world, those entities are transformed. More properly, for I do not wish to suggest that individuals are solely responsible for such transformations, once the sense of the society has been given substance and made literal by some individual genius, then we *know* what we only suspected before. And in the *Mona Lisa* we see suspicions take form. The famous enigmatic smile reveals a realm of privacy which we can glimpse but never know or possess, and the true individual is born. But the individual is created by pulling significance inward, and nature retreats outward as the thing we know as landscape. Of the *Mona Lisa*, van den Berg says:

The landscape behind her is justly famous; it is the first landscape painted as a landscape, just because it was a landscape. A pure landscape, not just a backdrop for human actions: nature, nature as the middle ages did not know it, an exterior nature closed within itself and self-sufficient, an exterior from which the human element has, in principle, been removed entirely. It is things-in-their-farewell, and therefore is as moving as a farewell of our dearest. It is the strangest landscape ever beheld by human eyes.[2]

Rilke claimed that it 'is not the portrayal of an impression, it is not the judgment of a man on things at rest; it is nature coming into being, the world coming into existence, unknown to man as the jungle of an unknown island.'[3] The natural environment becomes discernible from this moment on. It is removed from the background and made into foreground, an object of consciousness. This is a significant transformation, and one which is requisite to the existence of an environmental crisis, not to mention an environmental movement. When nature becomes discernible as a separate thing, it can exist as an object of discussion. But the act of becoming discernible is also indicative of a transformation of the human context or background. Nature is no longer a part of that which defines our existence and which reveals the phenomena of daily life; it is transformed from a definer and revealer to a thing defined and revealed. It is set apart to be operated upon at centre stage, through the universal tool of purposive thought.

It is significant that this change occurs before any explicit elaboration. The change is clearly in the air, its existence revealed in the act of an artist and not in a conscious doctrine set forth for public debate. The debate finally occurs when this understanding is made literal by Galileo and his followers a full century after Leonardo, but it is important to note that the verbal explication follows the contextual transformation. The possibility of seeing nature as foreground is given by a cultural context, which then allows Galileo to describe effectively a world devoid of background and a world with the living creature removed. Without the annoying distortion of an organic context the 'real' objects of the world seem to stand forth clearly and distinctly. The early scientist can assume a world of foreground and play his spotlight on those pieces of matter that interest him. The method evolved was a means of accomplishing just this, a way of systematically constraining one's attention to particular pieces of reality, pieces uninterpreted by the context of the whole.

In a sense the goal of trying to study a world without organic distortion is not unlike the phenomenologist's attempt to 'bracket' the world of common sense. Indeed, it was Husserl's desire to create a new science, but it had to be a *new* one because the old one had fatal flaws, including a belief in its own neutrality. It believed it was context-free, that it had eliminated what I have referred to above as 'background.' But in fact what it did was substitute a new background for the old, a context of belief in a neutral world rather than a discovery that there is no context and the world is neutral. But the context required for science has to precede science, and nature has to be created before it can be studied. Science is the consequence, not the cause, of the transformation of consciousness which we have been discussing. This is why Heidegger reversed the assumed order of things, arguing that technology precedes science. For Heidegger, as we have noted earlier, technology is not simply the utilization of tools but the understanding of the world as a field *for* the use of tools. That is, the world is revealed in a particular way, as 'standing-reserve,' when we adopt the stance of technology. The mode of questioning we adopt will bear within it the kind of world we find ourselves in and will suggest the kinds of action that are appropriate. If a tract of land 'is challenged in the hauling out of coal and ore,' then 'the earth now reveals itself as a coal mining district, the soil as mineral deposit.'[4] The world we see is therefore revealed against a background of belief, without which it could not appear as it does. And against that background there is only one kind of reaction available to us – the search for problems and solutions, a search which seems so obviously right that it is difficult to imagine it as the consequence of a particular context of understanding. Yet as Gregory Bateson has argued, the emergence of this technique of purposive thought has been a very mixed blessing.[5] It has encouraged attention to particular details and provided a means for manipulation, but it does so at the expense of what he calls 'systemic wisdom' – knowledge of the whole from which the pieces subjected to purposive thought are pulled. It gives us a useful 'bag of tricks' that is expected to resolve each dilemma but that in fact exacerbates many: tall smoke-stacks and catalytic converters are clever inventions, but they do not address the core of the environmental crisis. It is not a question of our encountering the crisis and resolving it through technology. The crisis is not simply something we can examine and resolve. We *are* the environmental crisis. The crisis is a visible manifestation of our very being, like territory revealing the self at its centre. The environmental crisis is inherent in everything we believe and do; it is inherent in the context of our lives.

If an alien ecologist were able to observe human beings from afar, he would perhaps have some difficulty in comprehending the nature of the creature before him. It displays some of the attributes of the settled or K-type of organism, with enduring communities and parental protection, but also many of the opportunistic or R-type traits, such as rapid dissemination and occupancy of disturbed (even if self-disturbed) communities. In fact, the alien observer may be compelled to conclude that he is witnessing either an erratic and displaced being – an exotic – or one whose effective role is to disrupt organic communities. Such a role, while unusual, would certainly not be unknown to him, if he were a connoisseur of earth-life. For there are several species that manifest themselves periodically as cataclysmic events; they effectively set back succession and thereby assure themselves – and a variety of other species – of conditions favourable to a continued, low-density existence. The locust and the spruce budworm are agents of change and diversity, challenging climax communities and effecting an increase in the heterogeneity of community pattern. But even if the alien observer were content to consider our species to be of the locust type, and thus to take a kindly view of our destructiveness, he could not help being concerned at the scale and longevity of our disruption. For, unlike other such creatures, we seem to have maintained our plague phase so long that we threaten permanent destruction rather than a successional set-back. That is, we now appear as agents of entropy rather than as inadvertent champions of heterogeneity. Even so, the observer's diagnosis of our behaviour as locust-like seems entirely appropriate. That is the way we behave. And given the 'story' we have adopted, it is the only role we are able to perform. We are the global locust, however imperfectly we play our role.

Context and Meaning

Until now I have been using the term 'background' interchangeably with the more appropriate term 'context,' simply because it is more easily visualized as that which stands behind the important (foreground) action. But unfortunately background also implies a secondary or subservient role for that which is so designated. This is less likely to be implied by context, since we are at least vaguely aware of the importance of context in our discernment of meaning. Anyone who has tried to define an isolated word will know how much we rely on context for our understanding of words. In our earlier example of the smoker looking for an ashtray, it was the context of smoking that resulted in the constitution of the ashtray – the concave surface stands out against that background as the object of the search. Without context there is very little scope for understanding, and only that because there is a kind of generic context which gives us immediate access to approximate meanings. Heidegger speaks of a mutual context of understanding, something which must exist before there can be communication. We are able to learn a variety of languages, for example, because we all understand basically how language works. Without that understanding we could not communicate as we do. 'Men exist "within language" prior to their uttering sounds because they exist within mutual context of understanding, which in the end is nothing but Being itself.'[6] Much of the shared context is social, but we understand something of other life-forms as well.

To share a context is to know 'how it is supposed to go.' Thanks to our shared understanding of language, we are able to leave out a great deal. Although we are not normally aware of the omissions, we recognize them in special cases. It is striking how quickly the deaf can sign to one another, with the recipient nodding agreement as soon as the meaning is grasped. It is also surprising to watch jazz musicians, who easily achieve an extemporaneous harmony with no apparent planning or agreement, simply because they share a musical context which allows them to sense the right time for changes required to sustain pattern. Rightness is accessible to beings in context. It should not surprise us that populations of organisms can act in unison, for in a sense they must do so. Nor should even a predator-prey collaboration seem remarkable, for few beings are so closely interrelated. So intertwined is their existence that some northern peoples are said to use the same word to designate both wolf and caribou. This example may be apocryphal, but it would certainly be an appropriate verbal convention. This is an extreme case of interspecific involvement, but to some extent we share a context with many other species, and indeed with all life. Hence we are able to grasp some of the meaning of their lives as well, although not without considerable risk of error.

In the case of living beings it may be fair to say that there is nothing at all without context. Merleau-Ponty speaks of the 'biological meaning

of the situation' which 'opens the way to another type of intelligibility.'
But if we turn back towards perceptual experience,

*we notice that science succeeds in constructing only a semblance of subjectivity: it
introduces sensations which are things, just where experience shows that there
are meaningful patterns; it forces the phenomenal universe into categories which
make sense only in the universe of science. It requires that two perceived lines,
like two real lines, should be equal or unequal, that a perceived crystal should have
a definite number of sides, without realizing that the perceived, by its nature,
admits of the ambiguous, the shifting, and is shaped by its context.*[7]

Organisms function in context, in the *Umwelt* which is their life and
their reality. Nothing is divorced from the context of life, and yet that
context is – and must be – invisible to those dependent upon it.

When we say that an animal exists, that it has *a world, or that it* belongs *to a
world, we do not mean that it has a perception or objective consciousness of that
world. The situation which unleashes instinctive operations is not entirely articulate and determinate, its total meaning is not possessed, as is adequately shown
by the mistakes and the blindness of instinct. It presents only a practical significance; it asks for only bodily recognition; it is experienced as an 'open'
situation, and 'requires' the animal's movements, just as the first notes of a
melody require a certain kind of resolution, without its being known in itself, and
it is precisely what allows the limbs to be substituted for each other, and to be of
equal value before the self-evident demands of the task.*[8]

The sense of rightness guides the act of the organism, and that sense
derives from the context of the action pending. As the context is
transformed – as it is at intervals in an organism's life – that which will
be right will be similarly altered. To put it another way, the meaning
discerned will depend on the context of existence. The meaning of the
other will vary depending on the season of the year and the season of
being, so that at one time it will be companion, at another time invader,
and at other times essentially non-existent. Jacob von Uexküll has even
shown that a black spot can mean different things to a hungry frog than
to a satiated one – the mood changes the 'reading' of the world. Even
the smoker will not always find concave surfaces to be ashtrays. But these

are instances of specific contexts of action rather than of an overreaching context of existence, which is Being itself. We should recall R.D. Laing's observations on the use of language, cited earlier. He found that in saying 'the sky is blue,' we end up commenting on the details of 'sky' and of 'blue' while we take for granted that which makes it possible to consider anything at all: 'is.'

None of the things that are united by 'is' can themselves qualify 'is'. 'Is' is not this, that, or the next, or anything. Yet 'is' is the condition of the possibility of all things. 'Is' is that no-thing whereby all things are.[9]

The context upon which all is dependent is that which we take for granted: the 'is.' It is 'that whereby all things are.' And 'the condition of the possibility of anything being at all, is that it is in relation to that which it is not. That is to say, the ground of the being of all beings is the relation between them.'[10] That very givenness, the 'is' of our existence, is the context that we ignore, that we cannot live without, and that facilitates and limits all we do.

As we experience the world, so we act. We conduct ourselves in the light of our view of what is the case and what is not the case. That is, each person is a more or less naïve ontologist. Each person has views of what is, and what is not.[11]

This is essentially all I have suggested through the analogy of neotenous development. Each of us is indeed a naïve ontologist, which is the inevitable condition of a natural alien. But we are nevertheless enmeshed in context, just like our niche-bound neighbours. We should not construe flexibility of context as absence of context. There may not be an essence of man, but there are surely essences of man inherent in every contextual revision we attempt. At the moment our essence is environmental crisis, to give it one name. And so long as it remains transparent to us, we are given over to it, and our actions are very nearly as determinate as the finished beings we so frequently belittle. Man's freedom lies primarily in the choosing of his 'story,' rather than his actions within that story. And having once chosen a locust-story as his own, the apparent range of choice is delimited by that central theme; we can only choose what seems 'sensible' to a locust.

Relationship as Context

To return to the *Concise Oxford* one last time, we find 'context' defined as 'parts that precede or follow a passage and fix its meaning.' That is, the meaning of the main event is set by those around it. It may be viewed in isolation but it cannot be understood in isolation. In the passage cited above, Laing suggests that 'is' is 'the condition of the possibility of anything being at all' and that 'the ground of the being of all beings is the relation between them.' If one wishes to understand rather than simply isolate the object of attention, one cannot ignore the relationships entailed. Indeed, one might say that the relationships *are* the main event, and that we deceive ourselves in concentrating on the beings rather than on the relationship between them. In other words, the context of our lives is constituted by the network of relationships which we are committed to – the relationships are the constituents of the *Umwelt*. But imagine the effect of reversing the polarity of attention, so to speak, so that the bond of relationship is more significant than the end-points it joins. Regarding the relations as primary is like reversing figure and ground, like stressing Being over beings. But to do so is to make a considerable leap, one which would certainly complicate our understanding of our selves and our world, if we bear in mind that the kinds and number of relationships may vary in social vertebrates. That is, there seems to be a contrast between the situation we find in social insects, in which the various forms of individual are embodiments of particular roles and hence of particular relationships to the society and the world, and that of the social vertebrates in which each individual is in effect a sequence of relationships. Rather than the creation of different individual forms, there is a temporal transformation of each individual into different social beings. The world looks different at one age than another, not just because of the accumulation of experience, but because of the transformation of mood and meaning that places the individual in a slightly different context and makes him a different individual. Viewed in this way, an individual is not a thing at all, but a sequence of ways of relating: a panorama of views of the world. Concentration on those relationships, and on relationship in general, clearly constitutes a substantial alteration in our way of understanding the individual.

Relationship is inevitable; it is a condition of existence. But the context established and the meaning which can be discerned are conditional upon the kind and nature of the relationship. Given our social gestation, this is perhaps the most significant focus of concern, for the nature of the relationship established will determine the world-view that an individual will become. As we suggested earlier, the most concise and evocative exposition of relationship is that of Martin Buber. The way in which we address the other is all-important, for it sets the stage for all that follows. 'The world as experience belongs to the basic word I-It. The basic word I-You establishes the world of relation.'[12] This striving for relation is primary. Objects of sensation ('detail-perception'?) are of secondary importance, and 'the genesis of the thing is a late product that develops out of the split of the primal encounters, out of the separation of the associated partners – as does the genesis of the I. In the beginning is the relation – as the category of being, as readiness, as a form that reaches out to be filled, as a model of the soul; the *a priori* of relation; *the innate You.*'[13] It is tempting, though no doubt too facile, to suggest that the world that emerges at the speaking of 'I-It' is that revealed by Whitehead's faculty of presentational immediacy (detail-perception), and the one that is summoned forth by 'I-You' is what is accessible through causal efficacy (meaning-perception). For our purposes it is enough to note the significance of relatedness and the profound transformations that accompany any change in stance towards the world. Buber's descriptions not only underline the significance of relationship but also remind us that it is not only the world that is transformed. When we say 'It,' both we and the world are changed. But it is reversible, if we can learn to say 'You' instead – a possibility which may depend on our having had the opportunity to explore that avenue of existence during childhood. Buber also cautions that 'the man who has acquired an I and says I-It assumes a position before things but does not confront them in the current of reciprocity'[14] – a significant deficiency, since 'relation is reciprocity.'[15] In other words, such a man rejects relationship, and in so doing rejects the possibility of having a world at all. He is condemned to exile, a habitual stranger staring at the relations of others.

Put this way, we have a slight re-phrasing of an earlier point, that we are not *in* an environmental crisis, but *are* the environmental crisis. By the very stance we take we prohibit the possibility of being anything else. The situation in which we find ourselves is a consequence of our own choice of context, for we have adopted one which defines relationship to nature out of existence. We have denuded the world of subjects and thus foreclosed any possibility of reciprocity or relationship. And yet, although we strive to reduce the bonds of kinship, we cannot succeed. However much we try to constitute a neutral world, we are drawn back by the primacy of relationship, a requirement which the sane may conceal but which the insane cannot. The psychiatrist Harold Searles observed, more than twenty years ago now, that among his schizophrenic patients there was a preponderance of individuals who had experienced difficulty in establishing enduring links with the non-human world. But 'it is not,' he says, 'that the "normal" culture member is so very different from the schizophrenic in this regard; it is that the "normal" person continuingly underestimates, or entirely overlooks, a fact which the schizophrenic simply cannot afford to ignore: the material objects in one's life are an emotionally meaningful part of it.'[16] Searles makes his debt to Buber explicit, agreeing that 'I-Thou' is the primary word of relation, and that 'the kind of relatedness which the mature human being experiences toward the nonhuman environment is identical with that relatedness which he experiences toward fellow human beings.'[17] He implies that the constitution of relatedness is an essential part of being human, and that we conceal or repress it at our peril. How, then, are we to make sense of this contradiction? If relationship is primary in our existence, why are we so committed to reducing the sensation of relatedness to earth?

It may be that this repression of relationship is simply one, and perhaps the easiest, of the options open to us as natural aliens. I use the term repression not in the formal sense, but as an analogy for the behaviour we manifest: it is *as if* we subconsciously repress any notion of involvement or kinship. Similarly, the earlier descriptions I have used might be regarded as analogies rather than explanations. They serve to sustain a platform of plausibility from which we can gain a different perspective. It is *as if* we were neotenic beings, craving meaning but condemned to search for it through the imperfect medium of culture. It is as if, in the course of our social gestation, those of us of western heritage have made the decision to substitute the more immediate rewards of detail-perception for the agonizing development of meaning-perception. It is as if, confused at the nature of our being, we have tried to piece together an image of what ought to be, without ever gaining a clear impression of the total composition. Our cultural undertaking has been something like trying to write an instruction manual for a child too insecure to try to ride its bicycle. And it is as if, in the constitution of an explanatory structure, we accidently amputated exactly that which we sought in the first place: the other half of our relationship. In deciding to annex subjectivity unto ourselves alone, we left nothing to relate to, no one else in the world to reciprocate. And thus it is as if we were locked into a particular manner of being, perhaps one analogous to the staring/objectification of the predatory mood, which prohibits the utterance that could transform us: 'You.'

Through our behaviour during our three-centuries-old endeavour to rid the planet of subjects – or to sever the vocal cords of the earth, to use an earlier metaphor – it is apparent which kind of stance we have chosen. Individualism is a religion of solitude. It is easier to live alone than to learn the constraints and obligations of community life. And what the environmental movement appears to protest – the extermination of other forms of life – is simply the physical manifestation of a global genocide that is long since accomplished in the minds of us all. The subjects are first destroyed, and later their bodies crumble. Our ability even to recognize the other had to be expunged if we were to live alone. The loss of the other bodies that roam the planet, things without subjectivity hanging in our icebox, followed inexorably. If we could deprive the smoker of his ability to conceive of ashtrays as effectively as we have removed our collective ability to constitute a world of subjects, the population of ashtrays would be similarly decimated. In effect, what cannot be conceived cannot exist – for us. And in this case, since what cannot exist is other subjects, the possibility of relationship is simultaneously diminished.

To some the loss of relationship with the non-human is compensated for by the abundance of humans. But it is apparent that relationship with other humans is also in jeopardy, and that we should not presume any firm boundary between our behaviour towards the human and towards the non-human: all 'others' are similarly threatened. Given our public posturings of concern for other people, this may not seem to be so. But that concern is somewhat illusory, a result of our ability to value the abstraction 'humanity' more than we do our concrete experience of other people. Hence the humanist can conjure up support for unknown groups of beleaguered people, just as the environmentalist can sometimes muster support for his own cherished abstractions, such as wilderness or natural harmony. These are clearly defences, and our need for them betrays our prior action in saying 'It' to the world and to each other. Even the call for an environmental ethic is an admission of this stance, for ethics in Anglo-American philosophy deals with the means of structuring the interactions of atomistic individuals. It is almost another technical fix, a cultural corrective to a congential deformity. But it also arises within a culture, and can only do, or even aim to do, what cultural assumptions reveal as possible. Given our choice of a subject-less world, it is unlikely that any amount of good intentions can diminish our consequences to the biosphere.

'The Eye altering alters all'

The magnitude of our dependence on unspoken assumptions has been a subject of perennial debate, and has been publicized by various individuals and groups. Two such groups have figured prominently in our earlier discussions. Both the Romantics and the phenomenologists have, despite the great diversity of their membership, been united in their attention to these assumptions, the 'real authorities' of a culture. In the case of the Romantics, there was a repeated emphasis on the importance of one's vantage-point in the understanding of the world. Indeed it was Newton's vantage-point, rather than any of his specific hypotheses or observations, that the Romantics responded to. 'What Coleridge and Wordsworth had said in their metaphors of creative perception, Shelley, like Blake, puts in a dramatic form: man's outlook does not merely reflect but alters his world.'[18] The world is transformed through the initial act of choosing, for 'the Eye altering alters all.'[19] The change in the individual prefigures a change in the world.

Those whom we categorize as phenomenologists – also a very diverse group – have elaborated a somewhat more structured and literal discussion of this phenomenon, although in comparison with other academic specialists their work may also seem poetic. Since much of the early work was done within the confines of philosophy proper, it is not surprising that there was an emphasis on comparing the new ideas with those of established philosophers. This makes the work somewhat inaccessible to the average reader, but even here there are reflections that bear directly on the question at hand. For instance, Husserl's objections to many of Kant's assumptions dominate some of his work, and cause Merleau-Ponty to comment as follows.

The best formulation of the [phenomenological] reduction is probably that given by Eugen Fink, Husserl's assistant, when he spoke of 'wonder' in the face of the world. Reflection does not withdraw from the world towards the unity of consciousness as the world's basis; it steps back to watch the forms of transcendence fly up like sparks from a fire; it slackens the intentional threads which attach us to the world and thus brings them to our notice; it alone is consciousness of the world because it reveals that world as strange and paradoxical. Husserl's transcendental is not Kant's and Husserl accuses Kant's philosophy of being 'worldly', because it makes use *of our relation to the world, which is the motive force of the transcendental deduction, and makes the world immanent in the subject, instead of* being filled with wonder *at it and conceiving the subject as a process of transcendence towards the world.*[20]

This contrast between making 'the world immanent in the subject' instead of 'being filled with wonder at it' summarizes rather well the two alternatives. What I have referred to as a rejection of relationship through the annexation of all subjectivity to the self is similar to regarding the world as immanent in the subject. The whole is annexed to the part. Against this view the phenomenologist posits an individual who is already in the world, and a situation in which it makes no sense to think of independent parts. Most significantly, however, he proposes a means of circumventing the determinants of perception and achieving some understanding independent of the 'natural attitude' that establishes a context and subtly shapes our experience. Within any context there is a self-consistency which affords us a sensation of truth. But the side-stepping of that context is the essential first step in achieving any re-evaluation, and this is precisely the action recommended by both the Romantics and the phenomenologists. The benefits of such side-stepping are also described in rather similar terms by both groups. Merleau-Ponty speaks of phenomenology as 'a transcendental philosophy which places in abeyance the assertions arising out of the natural attitude, the better to understand them; but it is also a philosophy for which the world is always "already there" before reflection begins – as an inalienable presence; and all its efforts are concentrated upon re-achieving a direct and primitive contact with the world, and endowing that contact with a philosophical status.'[21] This is put more simply by a *New York Times* writer who says that 'phenomenology could be described as a technique for discovering what is hidden in appearances by looking at the world through the eyes of an infant.'[22] Compare this with Shelley's claim that a function of his poetry is to purge 'from our inward sight the film of familiarity which obscures from us the wonder of our being ... It creates anew the universe.'[23] One ought not assume too great a similarity between the two groups, but in this respect at least they seem at one. Of the Romantics M.H. Abrams says:

The persistent enterprise is to make the old world new not by distorting it, but by defamiliarizing the familiar through a refreshed way of looking upon it. The prime opponent-power is 'custom' – what Wordsworth in The Prelude *repeatedly condemns as 'habit,' 'use and custom,' 'the regular action of the world' – which works insidiously and relentlessly to assimilate the unique existent to general perceptual categories. The result of overcoming this 'lethargy of custom,' Coleridge says, is to disimprison the 'wonder' in the 'familiar'; or in Wordsworth's alternative term, to reveal the miracle in the sheer existence of an object ...*[24]

The response of both groups to the threat of 'custom' or the 'natural attitude' is to counsel wonder. Or to put it the other way around, the consequence of evading the impact of constricting the world to one habitual brand of reality is the attainment of wonder at the familiar. Relieved of the cultural context which declares that *this* is important and *that* is not – a 'structure of meaningful distinctions,' to recall Douglas's comment about any environment we know – one is simply aware of what is. Wonder is the absence of interpretation.

I raise this point about the shared emphasis on the circumventing of cultural imperatives and the achievement of wonder in the face of the world partly to underline the importance of context as a determinant of the range of action open to a society and partly out of a kind of defensiveness. Throughout this discussion it has been my intention simply to identify whatever threads in the fabric of our social context are discernible and to ask how else we may manage to constitute an understanding of ourselves in the world. I have aspired only to ask 'what if?' – not to prescribe some splendid alternative which would solve all our perceived problems. In fact, even to deal in terms of problems and solutions would defeat my purpose, since it is my contention that it is thinking in such terms that characterizes our conventional world-view and condemns us to continue in this path of existence. But analysis alone is seldom considered an adequate goal. It is one of the presumptions of publishers and readers alike that once an analysis is attempted, it must be resolved through a solution. Hence, all is transformed into these two categories, problem and solution, and the world again congeals into an indifferent equation. My dilemma is that I must either disappoint the reader or contradict my own argument. An entirely unsatisfactory compromise suggests itself: I shall propose an entirely unsatisfactory solution. Unsatisfactory, that is, to anyone who demands immediate physical response to any perceived threat or imbalance. But to those who share the view that any dilemma is but a small manifestation of an entire social context, small beginnings may not seem futile – even if that beginning is only a defence of wonder.

A prerequisite to wonder is loss of complacency. Before anything can be experienced as wonderful, one must resist the temptation to dismiss it as nothing but something else, that is, as something 'unwonderful.' If the world is nothing but the machinations of energy exchange, then it is understood as such, and not as a source of wonder. True, the explanations of science may amaze us, but to say 'gee whiz' is not the same as to exclaim 'Oh!' They indicate qualitatively different experiences, admiration instead of awe. But the presence of explanation, even anticipated explanation, transforms the experience from wonder to quizzical bemusement or indifference. Gaston Bachelard claims:

A scientific worker has a discipline of objectivity that precludes all daydreams of the imagination. He has already seen what he observes in the microscope and, paradoxically, one might say that he never sees anything for the first time. In any case, in the domain of scientific observation that is absolutely objective, the 'first time' doesn't count. Observation, then, belongs to the domain of 'several times.' In scientific work, we have first to digest our surprise psychologically.[25]

To achieve a sense of wonder is to be continually surprised. It is tantamount to suspending all assumptions. It is to start over again.

For an adult it is impossible to sustain wonder for long, although it may be possible to entertain it often. It can be deliberately encouraged, and to do so is to re-enact, on an individual level, a singular event of the human past. For the experience of wonder is a cultural analogue of the neotenous origins of our species. Just as we were released from the dead-end of primate phylogeny to start again as beginners in life, we are released through wonder from our prison of preconceptions. Wonder suspends cultural imperatives just as neoteny suspends phylogenetic ones. This is not to suggest that culture may be indefinitely restrained, for we require a cultural resolution. 'Culture is the hypothesis we seek,' according to José Ortega y Gasset.[26] But the diversity of hypotheses that have existed bears witness to the range of alternative 'stories' we could have adopted as our own. The ability to change direction abruptly is given to only a few organisms, those with a rapid mutation rate and the one with an 'unfinished script.' For us wonder is a harbinger of hope, since it reminds us of our ability to suspend belief. If we were to do so, and if the new story we subsequently elaborated no longer casts us in the role of global locust, then our essence would no longer be environmental crisis. But there is no way to deliberately elaborate a new story – it is not a conscious exercise, not something susceptible of reasoned solution. One can only hope to pull back and see what emerges to fill the void. If we wonder, what shall we believe when we emerge from reverie? That is something each of must explore alone, before there can even emerge a vocabulary adequate to the elaboration of a new 'way the world is.'

If what we are is entailed in the story we create for ourselves, then only a new story will alter us and our actions. We cannot write a new story. But we can listen for one, once we recognize the need. And if we can side-step the protective barriers of common sense, there is the possibility that we can become fertile ground for a new start, a new story, and a redefining of our place in the world.

Obviously, such an observation is entirely inadequate to satisfy those who crave action and immediate, visible change. But to recommend action is to presume an end, and we do not have one. The only end at the moment is the massive proliferation and expansion that our locust-story requires; this is all that 'makes sense' (that is, is internally consistent). One cannot tack on a new conclusion to an old story, but one can be part of the genesis of a new understanding or approximation. Whether the alternative created will be better is something we can never know: it will only be different. In encouraging wonder we simply prepare the ground for the public germination of an idea that may have lain dormant, or semidormant, in our society for a very long time. The occasional flowerings we have observed suggest that this is so, although the ravings of the Romantics may never seem significant to the dedicated activist. But in fact, such anomalies are probably essential prerequisites to new action, for the activist can only make literal what has already been whispered in metaphor. 'Human life,' says Ortega, is 'a poetic undertaking, the invention of that character that each person, each epoch, has to be. Man is his own novelist.'[27]

I intimated earlier that one of the most potent weapons to be used against the environmental movement has been the term 'environmentalist.' This is not simply because it is a means of categorizing people and assigning arbitrary goals to them (which can then act as straw men to be knocked down by even the most witless of critics) but because it encourages us to consider the environmentalists' concern within the categories of contemporary thought. If the environmentalist is only concerned about a thing – environment – then that concern is easily resolved, either by safeguarding and repairing that thing, or by showing that it is of no consequence. But environmentalism, in the deepest sense, is *not* about environment. It is not about things but relationships, not about beings but Being, not about world but the inseparability of self and circumstance. In talking about the mountain the environmentalist seems to be defending a physical entity. But implicitly and emotionally he or she protests the categorization of 'mountain' – protests the isolation of portions of the world *as* things to defend or consume. The environmentalist resists the circumstance that makes it necessary to talk about 'environment' at all, and the first effective action he or she may take is to refute all association with that term and its derivatives. Not only would this thwart the efforts of opponents to impose a rationale upon the movement; it would also force each environmentalist to think clearly about his or her basic concern. Through such reflection the ecologist may remember that he was motivated initially by his irrepressible wonder at the existence of life, and the wilderness defender may remember that it was his experience, not real estate, that prompted his concern. Each may remember that the act of dissension implicit in the decision to declare himself entailed an understanding of the mis-fit between institutional reality and the experience of value. Each of us is, indeed, a naïve ontologist, although we often forgo our responsibility and simply let someone else – what people think – do it for us. And each of us must bear the responsibility if the public 'story' becomes one we cannot live through. Joseph Campbell speaks of a 'creative mythology' which each individual must take part in:

Creative mythology, in Shakespeare's sense, of the mirror 'to show virtue her own feature, scorn her own image, and the very age and body of the time his form and pressure,' springs not, like theology, from the dicta of authority, but from the insights, sentiments, thought, and vision of an adequate individual, loyal to his own experience of value. Thus it corrects the authority holding to the shells of forms produced and left behind by lives once lived. Renewing the act of experience itself, it restores to existence the quality of adventure, at once shattering and reintegrating the fixed, already known, in the sacrificial creative fire of the becoming thing that is no thing at all but life, not as it will *be* or as it *should be, as it* was *or as it* never *will be, but as it* is, *in depth, in process,* here and now, *inside and out.*[28]

To correct 'the authority holding to the shells of forms produced and left behind' is what any reformer would wish to accomplish. But shells are fiercely clung to and defended. Like hermit crabs, who protect their delicate abdomens by confiscating the shells of snails, we crawl into a structure of belief and refuse to expose ourselves, even to move to a more adequate abode. This is a dangerous policy. Some crabs are addicted to the shells of molluscs which are themselves extinct, and one must suspect that the crabs will soon follow suit unless they experience a change of aesthetic. The analogy is an obvious one, but what is equally obvious is that we do have a choice. In one sense, we are compromised by our dependence on artificial exoskeletons of thought and discourse. We cannot create a shell from within, strictly speaking. Gaston Bachelard has discussed the observation that

> *a shell carved by a man would be obtained from the outside, through a series of enumerable acts that would bear the mark of touched-up beauty; whereas 'the mollusk exudes its shell,' it lets the building material 'seep through,' 'distill its marvelous covering as needed.' And when the seeping starts, the house is already completed.*[29]

No shell seeps through to support a natural alien. The contrivance which sustains its existence is an approximation of that vestigial shell which no longer emerges to shape and support its being on earth. It is the responsibility of each of us to examine it at intervals and see what manner of creature we have become. Are we really what we think we are? Does this form actually embody the creature that we will to be, or is it some grotesque mask that conceals us from ourselves? As a first step outside the shell the environmentalist could shed his own label. Many other names and beliefs may be simultaneously dislodged, and then, just possibly, he can begin to glimpse the creature he might be. And if, a century hence, our descendants have as much difficulty in comprehending resources or benefit-cost analyses or environmental impact assessments as we have in understanding the significance of the philosopher's stone or the holy grail, then and only then will the environmental crisis have ceased to be. The persons involved in the environmental movement may have an important role to play if such a transformation is to occur. But many familiar and commonsensical things will crumble in the process. The demise of 'environmentalist' may be a first step in the cultural mutation.

Epilogue

The shrewd animals notice that we're not very much at home in this world we've expounded.

Rainer Maria Rilke

Embodied Limits

We began these reflections by considering the phenomenon of environmental defence and the difficulty inherent in 'talking about the mountain.' Since the beginnings of the contemporary environmental movement the number of persons moved to attempt that defence seems to have grown exponentially. Today, environmental platitudes drip from most political tongues, and even international bureaucracies are eager to pronounce upon the fate of the earth. Yet with all the talk and good intentions, the dying continues. In the United States alone, 94 species are known to have gone extinct since Earth Day (1970), with another 11 presumed extinct and 3 others existing only in captivity.[1] At the outset, I suggested that many people have come to feel that little has changed since Rachel Carson raised our awareness. But that response may seem puzzling today, when even the political institutions of the industrialized world appear willing to endorse the cause of 'the environment.'

It might help, however, to conclude with a final overview of our environmental perceptions and with a reminder of what is fundamentally required of us. Even though it is the demise of earthly forests that elicits our concern, we must bear in mind that as culture-dwellers we do not

live so much in forests of trees as in forests of words. And the source of
the blight that afflicts the earth's forests must be sought in the word-
forests – that is, in the world we articulate, and which confirms us as
agents of that earthly malaise.

Let us consider a simple example, an instance of human–non-human
encounter which occurred a few years ago. A worker on a humane society hot line received a call from a woman complaining that there was a
squirrel in her yard. The worker waited for the problem to be articulated, and finally realized that it had been: there was a squirrel in *her*
yard. In the mind of that suburbanite, nature had no business trespass-
ing on private property. The pacifying voice on the hot line was of little
comfort, and her annoyance doubtless continues. There are some interesting facets to the complaint, however, the first being that the person
saw the squirrel at all – not that it was visible to her, but that it was
'worth seeing.' The squirrel was really of no consequence to her existence, but nevertheless she responded to it.

That may not seem unusual – the family dog will also react to the
sight of a squirrel in the yard it occupies. But the same dog will very
likely ignore the sparrow hopping across its path, for the sparrow does
not figure significantly in the canine *Umwelt.* The dog, like other creatures, makes a world out of pieces of the planet. That is, it 'notices' only
those elements which are significant to it, and it makes the selection
through a combination of sensory limitations, perceptual abilities, and
learned preferences.[2] But the essential point is that each world is a subset of global elements, a subset entirely sufficient to the constitution of a
life-world. Equally important, that which is not seen, effectively does not
exist. And in such blessed ignorance lies the possibility of cohabitation.
There is little risk of trespass in the world of placeful animals, for that
which is without meaning is without reality. The sparrow may safely
share space with the dog, since neither exists for the other.

But since we see both dog and sparrow in the same space, such mutual ignorance[3] seems hard to credit. Furthermore, there is a lingering
tendency to speak of a 'law of the jungle' which decrees that all creatures be in constant competition with one another. Yet biologists and
naturalists have long realized that that is a serious misrepresentation.
Indeed, the ecologist Paul Colinvaux has suggested that species are best
thought of as nature's means of *avoiding* competition. For whereas indi-

viduals of a single species may well find themselves in pursuit of the same food item, those of differing species do not, for the obvious reason that they have different needs and different perceptions: creatures that eat green berries are not in the least discomfited by those that eat red ones.[4] Colinvaux suggests that 'a species could be thought of as a morphological expression of the animal's way of life, its niche.'[5] Hence, a species is essentially a set of *embodied limits*, a means of complementary restraint which facilitates the stunning profusion of life-forms on earth. But because these limits are *embodied*, because the 'agreement' is written in flesh rather than ink, they are modifiable only in evolutionary terms. There is no possibility of the green-berry eater's 'deciding' to compete for the red ones, because in effect, there are no red berries in its world.

In illustrating the complementary existence of seemingly similar species, Colinvaux describes an episode in which British fishermen were demanding the elimination of two species of cormorant which were alleged to be decimating their fish stocks. Upon investigation, it became apparent that not only did the two species select entirely different foods for themselves, but neither ate anything of significance to the human fishermen. What is especially interesting is the assumption of competition, the human expectation that other creatures are going to steal 'our' fish.[6]

The cormorants are spared that paranoia, not only by virtue of differing appetites but also, we might say, by ignorance of the possibility of a different diet. Their effective blindness to that which is not of their world rules out the very possibility of interspecies confrontation. But if that perceptual defect could be corrected through some optical technology, we would have, in effect, an instant 'sight-mutation' and the transformation of the species. Immediately, the cormorant's world would expand: what had been invisible would be made manifest, and open to exploration and occupancy. Again, I am speaking figuratively – the simple ability to see is not really what we are talking about, but rather the ability to find significance, something meaningful to the creature and therefore available to it. In 'correcting' its blindness, we have removed a biologically given limit: we have freed the animal from its contract to occupy this place, and have opened the way to its annexation of another.

That is precisely the temptation that the natural alien faces in the course of constituting a cultural world. We are able to 'make something of' objects which, strictly speaking, need not concern us; what in the world is a terrestrial primate doing fretting over fish in the North Atlantic? The 'gaps' which permit the red berries to fall out of the world of the green-berry eater are plugged by words. Both the berries and their perceivers remain behind as resources in the human word-world. Hence we constitute a single world where once there was a multitude.[7]

This translation of all entities into human objects is accomplished through the mediation of symbols. For while we are prone to think of our perception of the world as being a simple two-way association in which our eye captures an image of what is 'out there,' we tend to ignore the important third dimension: that what is out there is immediately named, and thus transformed from direct experience to human abstraction. And as Walker Percy has pointed out, what is especially significant is that anything can be named – even gaps.[8] We name not only those plants which are of direct utility, but all the rest as well, even if only as 'bush' (which, upon a discovery of its usefulness, can become a 'resource'). What we witness, in the modern elaboration of the natural alien, is the collapse of the multi-layered world of nature, the overlapping *Umwelten* which interpenetrate but never touch, into a single spatial pancake which we claim as our own.

George Steiner once observed that 'language is the main instrument of man's refusal to accept the world as it is.'[9] Through this particular act of translation, the pattern of millions of years of organic evolution is reversed. The efflorescence of forms of being, of embodied limits, is challenged by a dramatic sight-mutation. The moment we can name and therefore possess the objects of another's world, we are able to enucleate that creature's life-world and annex the remains.

Conservation

Two obvious consequences of the perception of a global niche are the presumption of universal competition – cormorants eating 'our' fish – and the quest to legitimate that perception through ever-greater control (i.e., technological appropriation). Environmental defenders are quick to criticize the actions of those who pursue that quest without regard to its consequences. But ironically, the environmentalists' vision of a unified planet, symbolized by images of Earth as seen from outer space, only helps legitimate the quest for control in the guise of 'global management.' If what is at stake is the fate of the planet, then any intervention seems justified.[10] Thus, rather than diminish the appetite for domination of the natural world, the environmental crisis has served to sanction virtually any activity which embraces the cause of planetary survival.

But although the scale of our presumption is novel, the response to the perception of environmental malaise is surely not. Around the turn of the century, for example, there was a growing realization that the forests of the United States were not limitless and were suffering from flagrant over-exploitation. The prominent forester Gifford Pinchot advocated a system of 'conservation' to help sustain forest production. But it is interesting that the expressions he used in articulating his concern are still largely applicable – although he was less circumspect about his intentions than we are today. He proclaimed, for example, that 'the first duty of the human race is to control the earth it lives upon.'[11]

Conservation, he claimed, entails the same attitude towards nature as the businessman holds towards his business. It entails 'prudence and foresight' rather than recklessness; it requires that resources be public property and not be closeted in private monopolies; and it 'demands the complete and orderly development of all our resources for the benefit of all the people.' Finally, conservation entails a recognition of the rights of the present generation to use all it wants of the natural resources available, along with an obligation to preserve some for future generations.[12]

That sounds distinctly familiar. Notice the emphasis on conservation as an economic activity, on nature as a collection of resources for human use, on resources being used for the benefit of all, and on the inevitability of development. We can see how strangely contemporary such assertions are if we compare them with the following:

Humanity has the ability to make development sustainable – to ensure that it meets the needs of the present without compromising the ability of future generations to meet their own needs. The concept of sustainable development does not imply limits – not absolute limits but limitations imposed by the present state of

*technology and social organization on environmental resources and by the ability
of the biosphere to absorb the effects of human activities. But technology and
social organization can be both managed and improved to make way for a new
era of economic growth.*[13]

That is the most recent invocation of Pinchot's conservation philosophy, as expressed by the Brundtland Commission's popular report, *Our
Common Future.*[14] The similarities are striking: Pinchot calls for use of
nature by all Americans, Brundtland, by all humans; both treat the
world as a single niche; both insist that development is essential; and
both reject the very possibility of limits, for, in Pinchot's words, 'the
first great fact about conservation is that it stands for development.'[15]
Development has come to seem the universal solution to any and all
difficulties, a term which, though amorphous enough to accommodate
almost any definition, achieves a sense of naturalness and inevitability
because of its original biological meaning – the orderly growth and elaboration of an organism in the course of its genesis. Hence, as the German researcher Wolfgang Sachs has observed, through the trick of using
this biological metaphor 'a simple economic activity turns into a natural
and evolutionary process, as though hidden qualities would be progressively developed to their final state. The metaphor thus says that the real
destiny of natural goods is to be found in their economic utilization; all
economic uses are a step forward to direct inner potential toward that
goal.'[16] Development thus understood seems almost a moral imperative.

Both Brundtland and Pinchot articulate the position of the occupant
of the global niche; as Pinchot has reputedly said, there are only two
things in the world, people and resources.[17] Our more subtle reworkings
of that assertion do not diminish its underlying premise concerning the
total dedication of the planet to human purposes – or rather to the
contemporary human economy. Sachs concludes that the 'redefinition
of the indictment of growth – presenting it as a problem of conserving
resources – defused the conflict between growth and environment and
turned it into a managerial exercise.'[18]

The admonition to conserve the world amounts, then, to an acceptance that it be subverted wholly to our purposes through global
development. And to promote 'sustainable development' is to sanitize

semantically the habitual project of planetary domestication and to provide a sense of salvation without the discomfort of authentic change. To be able to speak of the globe as 'our environment' permits us to reinforce the notion of a single, human world and consequently to place ourselves in direct confrontation with virtually every other life-form.

That is not to malign the intentions of the advocates of such measures, but instead to highlight the cultural context which subverts those intentions by covertly insinuating a belief in the necessity of human domination and control. One certainly must admire, for example, the efforts made by thousands of dedicated people to protect endangered species. Yet even in that endeavour, a paradox immediately emerges: if, to save the California condor, it is necessary to imprison every extant example of that being, what have we saved? A singular bird, certainly, but one which can be regarded as saved only by accepting a limited, biological definition of a bird as the physical manifestation of coded genetic information. Were it regarded as the manifestation of embodied limits and therefore the functionary of a particular 'place,' the fact that we have expertly exterminated that place makes nonsense of any claims that the bird has been saved. Hence, Charles Bergman's conclusion that 'the problem of endangered species is only superficially a biological problem. Endangered species are the inevitable expression of our power over nature.'[19] The centrality of that power over nature is hidden from us by our good intentions, but the upshot of our efforts to save is usually the increase in our own dominion and the disempowerment of our designated wards. Even without visible confinement, the remnant individuals are contained by observation and manipulation, until they are mere data on our maps. The wild beasts of the forests, radio-collared and drained of their secrets, are little more than unruly livestock on long leashes.

Christopher Lasch has suggested that 'progressive optimism rests, at bottom, in a denial of the natural limits on human power and freedom, and it cannot survive for very long in a world in which an awareness of those limits has become inescapable.'[20] Yet it is remarkable how skilfully we repress such awareness. And when a group such as the Brundtland Commission, established because of the pressure of impending limitation, is able to assert that 'sustainable development does not imply limits,' we must wonder what hope remains.

Doubt and Faith

The redefinition of earth as human-owned space entails the elimination
of the concept of place – nothing 'belongs' anywhere. Yet in a manner
of speaking, that amounts to an act of global extinction, for if place
goes, so too do the beings made to it. Remember, an animal is not only a
body; it is embodied limits, which means the functionary of a place in
the planetary biosphere. The body is merely the contract, the 'deed' to
place. One might say that the place *is* the species, for the place is more
real and enduring than flesh. But 'environment' does not harbour
place. Environment is not a life-world, but simply a surrounding. Indeed
it is not a 'thing' at all, but a statement of anthropocentricity: the planet, now expropriated as ours alone, is our surrounding, our environment. But Sachs presses the issue further:

*What does the environment surround? What is important about it and for
whom? In the usage of international environmental reports, the hidden subject is
usually nothing other than the national economy. Environment appears as the
sum total of physical barriers hampering the dynamics of the economic system.*[21]

In other words, 'our' environment comes to be seen not even as the
surroundings of people, but as the surroundings of an economy of
which we are functionaries. It is merely the support-base of that system
of human organization. Hence, nature is 'edited' to become 'the
environment,' or whatever surrounds and supports that system. This is
the grand insight of the Brundtland Commission: 'In the past we
have been concerned about the impact of economic growth upon the
environment; we are now forced to concern ourselves with the impact of
ecological stress upon our economic prospects.'[22]

In the sequence of sight-mutations which has given rise to our present
understanding of ourselves and of nature, we have relinquished the
subject-generated sense of place in favour of the abstraction of universal
space, which, in turn, facilitates the notion of a single world with universal competition. The revolts against this vision, from Romanticism to
the early stages of the environmental movement, have been attempts to
reassert the experience of the earth as a heterogeneous mosaic of places, and of subjects as place-limited participants in the planet.

As symbol-using social beings, we are vulnerable to conceptual salta-
tion, and it is not at all surprising that we vary so much from group to
group and over time. George Steiner observed that 'ours is the ability,
the need, to gainsay or "un-say" the world, to image and speak it
otherwise.'[23] What is troublesome about our present situation is the
simplification and homogenization of world-view which has occurred,
and the consequent loss of contrasting 'hypotheses' with their attendant
perceptions.[24]

But if, as I have attempted to show, traces of contrasting understandings remain even within this monolithic culture, perhaps there is still
the possibility of an internal challenge, an attempt to 'un-say' our
present world. Phenomenology, with its explicit shunning of explanations and constructs, might usefully be regarded as a means of unplug-
ging the gaps which we have filled with words and symbols, so as to
focus on that which is humanly significant and let the rest slip past for
the habitation of others. To 'bracket' is to set aside those obstructions,
and the pre-cognitive life-world that the phenomenologist seeks may
constitute our closest approximation of the life-world of placeful beings.
Perhaps the goal, then, is again to 'embody limits' – to constitute a
culture-world that is self-limiting and thus to block the entropic absorp-
tion of all worlds into one.

Yet even if we could muster some optimism over the possibility of un-
saying the world, how could we recognize a viable alternative if we 'said'
it? How would we discern it as preferable? We would not, in all likeli-
hood; we will always harbour doubt. To Descartes, that doubt seemed a
proof of our existence – and, in effect, of the virtual non-existence of
non-doubters, that is, other animals. Doubt is a phenomenon rarely
faced by a placeful being; so too, belief. They are the coin of the natural alien, and we oscillate between them.

We are apt to dismiss our companions on this planet as instinct-
bound robots or prisoners of necessity. But perhaps instinct (a term
which signifies nothing but permits us to dismiss subjectivity)[25] is more
usefully regarded as faith, faith in the destiny that awaits the creature
who embodies limits, and faith in the utter propriety of the here and
now.

Somewhere in a forest stands a tree in which, sixty feet above the
ground, tiny wood duck nestlings struggle to an opening in the trunk,

and peer out at the ground below. Each flightless duckling steps into the abyss. All tumble to the ground and, if they survive, continue their pursuit of home. Their destination is a lake where, together with their parents, they will continue their privileged existence. No duck need declare itself master of its fate or captain of its soul; the faith that has sustained this expression of being for millennia permits the duckling to take its necessary step.

It is a faith that will continue to elude us; that too is the condition of the natural alien.[26] But if we could replace contempt with envy and acknowledge the strange superiority which our placeful companions enjoy, we might at least aspire to some cultural imitation of a life of 'embodied limits.'

Henry Beston has argued that we need a wiser concept of animals:

We patronize them for their incompleteness, for their tragic fate of having taken form so far below ourselves. And therein we err, and greatly err. For the animal shall not be measured by man. In a world older and more complete than ours they move finished and complete, gifted with extension of the senses we have lost or never attained, living by voices we shall never hear. They are not brethren, they are not underlings; they are other nations, caught with ourselves in the net of life and time, fellow prisoners of the splendor and travail of the earth.[27]

Far from being tragic cripples, unable to aspire to the heights open to humans, those 'other nations' constitute a source of hope, for they are portentous evidence of the only successful experiment in living ever conducted on this planet. The way of differentiation and limitation, forged through evolution, is celebrated daily in the profusion of place-ways which grace the earth. Would that we could embrace just one of those ways, and abandon the entropic project of planetary domination.

Notes

PREFACE

1 Lewis Mumford, *Technics and Human Development* (New York: Harcourt Brace Jovanovich 1967), p 16.
2 Paul Shepard, 'Whatever Happened to Human Ecology?' *Bioscience*, 17 (1967), 893.
3 Mary Douglas, 'Environments at Risk,' in Jonathan Benthall, *Ecology: The Shaping Enquiry* (London: Longman 1972), p 139.

CHAPTER ONE

1 Theodore Roszak, *Where the Wasteland Ends* (Garden City: Doubleday 1972), p 400.
2 For a thorough discussion of this theme see Clarence Glacken, *Traces on the Rhodian Shore* (Berkeley: University of California Press, 1967).
3 An excellent discussion can be found in Steven Fox, *John Muir and His Legacy: The American Conservation Movement* (Boston: Little, Brown 1981).
4 William Tucker, 'Is Nature Too Good for Us?' *Harper's* March 1982, pp 29, 35.
5 'Pesticides: The Price of Progress,' *Time*, 28 September 1962, p 69. For a later discussion see *Time*, 2 September 1970.
6 Anthony Brandt, 'Views,' *The Atlantic Monthly*, July 1977, p 49.

7 John Livingston, *The Fallacy of Wildlife Conservation* (Toronto: McClelland & Stewart 1981), p 33.

8 David Ehrenfeld, *The Arrogance of Humanism* (New York: Oxford University Press 1978), p 210.

9 Henry David Thoreau, cited in Donald Worster, *Nature's Economy: The Roots of Ecology* (New York: Anchor 1979), p 95.

10 This phrase is borrowed from Nelson Goodman, 'The Way the World Is,' *Review of Metaphysics*, 14 (1960), 48–56.

11 See Catherine Roberts, *The Scientific Conscience* (New York: Braziller 1967), pp 41–2, for this and other examples.

12 Claude Bernard, cited in John Vyvyan, *In Pity and in Anger* (London: Michael Joseph 1969), p 43.

13 Claude Bernard, *An Introduction to the Study of Experimental Medicine* (New York: Dover 1957), p 103.

14 Vyvyan, *In Pity and in Anger*, p 132.

15 See Max Horkheimer, *Critical Theory: Selected Essays* (New York: Herder & Herder 1972), p 152. I am endebted to Douglas Torgerson for drawing this reference to my attention.

16 S. Drake, ed and trans, *Discoveries and Opinions of Galileo* (Garden City: Doubleday 1957), p 274.

17 Ludwig von Bertalanffy, 'An Essay on the Relativity of Categories,' *Philosophy of Science*, 22:4 (1955), 258.

18 J.H. van den Berg, *The Changing Nature of Man: Introduction to a Historical Psychology* (New York: Delta 1975), p 69.

19 Robert Henry Peters, 'From Natural History to Ecology,' *Perspectives in Biology & Medicine*, 24 (1979), 191.

20 Peters, 'Natural History to Ecology,' p 192.

21 Worster, *Nature's Economy*, p 301.

22 Worster, *Nature's Economy*, p 302.

23 Peters, 'Natural History to Ecology,' p 202.

24 Worster, *Nature's Economy*, p 315.

25 Peters, 'Natural History to Ecology,' p 193.

26 Worster, *Nature's Economy*, p 304.

27 R.D. Laing, *The Politics of Experience* (Harmondsworth: Penguin 1967), pp 51–2.

28 William Leiss, 'Nature as a Commodity: Landscape Assessment and the Theory of Reification,' unpublished manuscript.

29 E.H. Gombrich, *Norm and Form* (London: Phaidon 1966); see especially ch 9, pp 107–21.

30 William Leiss, *The Domination of Nature* (Boston: Beacon 1974).

31 E.F. Schumacher, *A Guide for the Perplexed* (New York: Harper Colophon 1977), p 1.

32 Schumacher, *Guide*, p 4.

33 Arne Naess, 'The Shallow and the Deep Long Range Ecology Movement,' introductory lecture, Third World Future Research Conference, Bucharest, 3–10 September 1972. A discussion of this topic can be found in Sigmund Kvaløy, 'Ecophilosophy and Ecopolitics: Thinking and Acting in Response to the Threats of Ecocatastrophe,' *The North American Review*, 260 (Summer 1974), 17–28.

34 William Devall, 'The Deep Ecology Movement,' *Natural Resources Journal*, 20:1 (April 1980), 299.

35 Arne Naess, 'The Place of Joy in a World of Fact,' *The North American Review*, 259 (Summer 1973), 55.

36 Devall, 'Deep Ecology,' p 317.

37 Naess, 'Place of Joy,' p 55.

38 Kvaløy, 'Ecophilosophy and Ecopolitics, pp 17–28.

39 Devall, 'Deep Ecology,' p 310.

40 Worster, *Nature's Economy*, p 82.

41 M.H. Abrams, *Natural Supernaturalism: Tradition and Revolution in Romantic Literature* (New York: Norton 1971), p 260.

42 F. Schiller, cited in Abrams, *Natural Supernaturalism*, p 261.

43 Roszak, *Wasteland*, pp 278–345.

44 Robert Combs, *Vision of the Voyage* (Memphis: Memphis State University Press 1978), pp 29–30.

45 Combs, *Vision*, p 30.

46 Combs, *Vision*, p 2.

47 Alfred North Whitehead, *Science and the Modern World* (New York: The Free Press 1967), p 81.

48 Combs, *Vision*, p 1.

49 Abrams, *Natural Supernaturalism*, p 341.

50 Whitehead, *Science and the Modern World*, p 83.

51 Whitehead, *Science and the Modern World*, p 84.

52 Whitehead, *Science and the Modern World*, p 93.

CHAPTER TWO

1 Paul Shepard, 'Whatever Happened to Human Ecology?' *Bioscience*, 17 (1967), 893.

2 For a thorough treatment see Peter Berger and Thomas Luckman, *The Social Construction of Reality* (New York: Anchor Books 1967).

3 See Stephen Fox, *John Muir and His Legacy: The American Conservation Movement* (Boston: Little, Brown 1981).

4 John Fowles, 'Seeing Nature Whole,' *Harper's*, November 1979, p 50.

5 See Lewis Thomas, *Lives of a Cell* (New York: Bantam Books 1974).

6 D. Reanny, 'Extrachromasomal Elements as Possible Agents of Adaptation and Development,' *Bacteriological Review*, 40 (1976), 552–90.

7 WNED, 'The Dick Cavett Show,' 3 August 1979.

8 This topic is discussed by Edward T. Hall in *Beyond Culture* (New York: Anchor 1976).

9 Maurice Merleau-Ponty, *Phenomenology of Perception* (London: Routledge & Kegan Paul 1962), pp 148–9.

10 Merleau-Ponty, *Phenomenology*, p 77.

11 William Barrett, *Irrational Man* (New York: Anchor 1962), p 217.

12 Merleau-Ponty, *Phenomenology*, pp xvi–xvii.

13 Merleau-Ponty, *Phenomenology*, pp 140–1.

14 Merleau-Ponty, *Phenomenology*, p 146.

15 See, for example, Jakob von Uexküll, 'A Stroll Through the Worlds of Animals and Men,' in Claire Schiller, ed, *Instinctive Behavior* (New York: International Universities Press 1957), pp 5–80.

16 John H. Hanson, 'René Descartes and the Dream of Reason,' in Marie Coleman Nelson, ed, *The Narcissistic Condition* (New York: Human Sciences Press 1977), p 175.

17 Sigmund Freud, cited in J.H. van den Berg, *The Changing Nature of Man* (New York: Delta 1975), p 234.

18 Van den Berg, *The Changing Nature of Man*, p 235.

19 Merleau-Ponty, *Phenomenology*, p xi.

20 Merleau-Ponty, *Phenomenology*, pp 431–2.

21 Robert Combs, *Vision of the Voyage* (Memphis: Memphis State University Press 1978), p 2.

22 Marjorie Hope Nicolson, *Mountain Gloom and Mountain Glory: The Development of the Aesthetics of the Infinite* (Ithaca: Cornell University Press 1959), p 35.

23 Nicolson, *Mountain Gloom*, p 42.

24 Ronald Rees, 'The Taste for Mountain Scenery,' *History Today* 25 (1975), 306.

25 Nicolson, *Mountain Gloom*, p 1.

26 E.H. Gombrich, *Norm and Form* (London: Phaidon 1966), pp 117, 118.

27 Oscar Wilde, *De Profundis and Other Writings* (Harmondsworth: Penguin 1954), pp 78–9.

28 Samuel Y. Edgerton, Jr, *The Renaissance Rediscovery of Linear Perspective* (New York: Basic Books 1975), p 24.
29 Edgerton, *Renaissance Rediscovery*, p 30.
30 R.D. Laing, *The Politics of Experience* (Harmondsworth: Penguin 1967), p 24.
31 Ludwig von Bertalanffy, *Robots, Men, and Minds* (New York: Braziller 1967), pp 51–2.
32 Mary Warnock, *Existentialism* (Oxford: Oxford University Press 1970), p 39.
33 Alfred North Whitehead, *Science and the Modern World* (New York: The Free Press 1967), pp 54–5.

CHAPTER THREE

1 Mary Warnock, *Existentialism* (Oxford: Oxford University Press 1970), p 36.
2 See Paul Shepard, *Thinking Animals* (New York: Viking 1978).
3 Maurice Merleau-Ponty, *The Structure of Behavior* (Boston: Beacon 1963), p 3.
4 Maurice Merleau-Ponty, cited in Quentin Laurer, *The Triumph of Subjectivity* 2nd ed (New York: Fordham University Press 1978), p 7.
5 Erazim Kohák, *Idea and Experience* (Chicago: University of Chicago Press 1978), p 11.
6 R.D. Laing, *The Politics of Experience* (Harmondsworth: Penguin 1967), p 20.
7 John Wild, *Existence and the World of Freedom* (Englewood Cliffs: Prentice-Hall 1963), p 35.
8 Laing, *Politics*, p 35.
9 Martin Heidegger, *Being and Time* (New York: Harper & Row 1962), p 46.
10 Heidegger, *Being and Time*, p 51.
11 *Concise Oxford Dictionary*, 6th ed (London: Oxford University Press 1976), p 828.
12 Heidegger, *Being and Time*, p 54.
13 George Steiner, *Heidegger* (London: Fontana/Collins 1978), p 18.
14 Heidegger, *Being and Time*, pp 83–4.
15 William Barrett, *Irrational Man* (Garden City: Doubleday Anchor 1962), pp 218–19.
16 Wild, *Existence*, p 47.

17 Heidegger, *Being and Time*, p 93.

18 Heidegger, *Being and Time*, p 160.

19 Wild, *Existence*, pp 21–2.

20 Heidegger, *Being and Time*, p 94.

21 Heidegger, *Being and Time*, p 100.

22 Julian Marias, *Philosophy as Dramatic Theory* (University Park: Pennsylvania State University Press 1971), p 260.

23 Martin Heidegger, *Basic Writings*, ed Martin Krell (New York: Harper & Row 1977), p 299.

24 Steiner, *Heidegger*, p 134.

25 Heidegger, *Basic Writings*, p 328.

26 Joseph Grange, 'On the Way towards Foundational Ecology,' *Soundings*, 60:1 (1977), 136.

27 Grange, 'Foundational Ecology,' p 146.

28 Steiner, *Heidegger*, p 97.

29 Heidegger, *Basic Writings*, pp 234–5.

30 For a discusssion of environmental ethics and world-view see Don E. Marietta, Jr, 'Knowledge and Obligation in Environmental Ethics: A Phenomenological Approach,' *Environmental Ethics*, 4:2 (Summer 1982), 153–62.

31 Michael F. Zimmerman, 'Toward a Heideggerean Ethos for Radical Environmentalism,' *Environmental Ethics*, 5:2 (Summer 1983), 118.

32 Steiner, *Heidegger*, p 98.

33 Max Scheler, cited in E. Relph, *Place and Placelessness* (London: Pion 1976), p 43.

34 Maurice Merleau-Ponty, *Phenomenology of Perception* (London: Routledge & Kegan Paul 1962), p 23.

35 Steiner, *Heidegger*, p 69.

36 Stephen Fox, *John Muir and His Legacy: The American Conservation Movement* (Boston: Little, Brown 1981), p 335.

37 Steiner *Heidegger*, p 31.

38 Samuel Taylor Coleridge, *The Friend*, vol I, ed Barbara Rooke (London: Routledge & Kegan Paul 1969), p 514.

39 Heidegger, *Basic Writings*, p 221.

40 Martin Heidegger, cited in Arne Naess *Four Modern Philosophers* (Chicago: University of Chicago Press 1968), p 174.

CHAPTER FOUR

1 Nelson Goodman, 'The Way the World Is,' *Review of Metaphysics*, 14 (1960), 56.

2 Don E. Marietta, Jr, 'Knowledge and Obligation in Environmental Eth-

ics: A Phenomenological Analysis,' *Environmental Ethics*, 4:2 (Summer 1982), 157.

3 The term 'compliance' is borrowed from John Livingston, *The Fallacy of Wildlife Conservation* (Toronto: McClelland & Stewart 1981).

4 Edmund Leach, *Lévi-Strauss* (London: Fontana/Collins 1974), p 21.

5 Adolph Portmann, *Animals as Social Beings* (London: Hutchinson 1961), p 26.

6 Marjorie Grene, *Approaches to a Philosophical Biology* (New York: Basic Books 1968), p 28.

7 The significance of the amateur in the conservation movement is admirably illustrated in Stephen Fox's *John Muir and His Legacy: The American Conservation Movement* (Boston: Little Brown 1981).

8 This term was coined by Livingston in *The Fallacy of Wildlife Conservation*, p 92.

9 Jakob von Uexküll, 'A Stroll Through the Worlds of Animals and Men,' in Claire Schiller, ed, *Instinctive Behavior* (New York: International Universities Press 1957), p 6.

10 Uexküll, 'Stroll,' p 5.

11 Uexküll, 'Stroll,' p 11.

12 Maurice Nicoll, cited in E.F. Schumacher, *A Guide for the Perplexed* (New York: Harper Colophon 1977), p 33.

13 Maurice Merleau-Ponty, *Phenomenology of Perception* (London: Routledge & Kegan Paul 1962), p 430.

14 Grene, *Approaches*, p 173.

15 Uexküll, 'Stroll,' p 14.

16 Uexküll, 'Stroll,' p 29.

17 John Wild, *Existence and the World of Freedom* (Englewood Cliffs: Prentice-Hall 1963), pp 111–12.

18 Julian Marias, *José Ortega y Gasset: Circumstance and Vocation* (Norman: University of Oklahoma Press 1970), p 359.

19 Hans Jonas, *The Phenomenon of Life* (New York: Delta 1966), p 136.

20 Jonas, *Phenomenon of Life*, p 139.

21 Jonas, *Phenomenon of Life*, p 152.

22 John H. Hanson, 'René Descartes and the Dream of Reason,' in Marie Coleman Nelson, ed, *The Narcissistic Condition* (New York: Human Sciences Press 1977), pp 172–3.

23 Marshall McLuhan discusses the modifying effects of technology in most of his books, but the one he wrote with H. Parker, *Through the Vanishing Point* (New York: Harper & Row 1968), deals explicitly with vision and the effect of perspective in painting.

24 C.S. Lewis, cited by McLuhan and Parker, *Vanishing Point*, p 24.

25 Lionel Trilling, *Sincerity and Authenticity* (London: Oxford University Press 1974), p 24.

26 Trilling, *Sincerity*, pp 144–5.

27 McLuhan and Parker, *Vanishing Point*, p 13.

28 McLuhan and Parker, *Vanishing Point*, p 20.

29 William M. Ivins, Jr, *On the Rationalization of Sight* (New York: Da Capo 1973), p 13.

30 Susan Sontag, *On Photography* (New York: Farrar, Straus, & Giroux 1977), p 23.

31 Sontag, *On Photography*, p 97.

32 Yi-Fu Tuan, 'Structuralism, Existentialism, and Environmental Perception,' *Environment and Behavior*, 4:3 (September 1972), 330.

33 Tuan, 'Structuralism,' p 329.

34 Erwin Straus, *Phenomenological Psychology* (New York: Basic Books 1966), p 219.

35 Straus, *Phenomenological Psychology*, p 223.

36 Straus, *Phenomenological Psychology*, p 219.

37 Mary Midgley, *Beast and Man: The Roots of Human Nature* (New York: New American Library 1978), p 11.

38 Roger Callois, *The Mask of Medusa* (New York: Clarkson N. Potter 1964).

39 Midgley, *Beast*, p 12.

40 Barry Holstun Lopez, *Of Wolves and Men* (New York: Scribner's 1978), p 94.

41 Erazim Kohák, *Idea and Experience* (Chicago: University of Chicago Press 1978), p 81.

42 Grene, *Approaches*, p 21.

43 Grene, *Approaches*, p 23.

44 Grene, *Approaches*, p 24.

45 Adolph Portmann, *Animal Forms and Patterns: A Study of the Appearance of Animals* (New York: Schocken 1967), p 183.

46 Sontag, *On Photography*, p 11.

47 Ansel Adams, cited in Sontag, *On Photography*, p 118.

48 Minor White and Henri Cartier-Bresson, cited in Sontag *On Photography*, p 116.

49 For a different interpretation of Arbus's work see Sontag, *On Photography*, pp 32–42.

50 This term was coined by the western Canadian photographer and artist Harry Savage.

51 Sontag, *On Photography*, p 119.

52 Sontag, *On Photography*, p 117.
53 Sontag, *On Photography*, p 97.
54 Sontag, *On Photography*, p 111.
55 M.S. Friedman, cited in Harold Searles, *The Nonhuman Environment in Normal Development and in Schizophrenia* (New York: International Universities Press 1960), p 117.
56 Martin Buber, *I and Thou* (New York: Scribner's 1970), pp 58–9.
57 Eric Fromm, cited by Harold Searles, *The Nonhuman Environment*, p 393.
58 M.H. Abrams, *Natural Supernaturalism: Tradition and Revolution in Romantic Literature* (New York: Norton 1971), p 369.
59 Abrams, *Natural Supernaturalism*, p 366.
60 Abrams, *Natural Supernaturalism*, p 341.
61 Kathleen Raine, *Blake and the New Age* (London: George Allen & Unwin 1979), p 30.
62 Raine, *Blake*, p 29.

CHAPTER FIVE

1 E.F. Schumacher, *A Guide for the Perplexed* (New York: Harper Colophon 1977), p 51.
2 Schumacher, *Guide*, pp 52–3.
3 Schumacher, *Guide*, p 61.
4 Schumacher, *Guide*, p 61.
5 Colin Wilson, *Beyond the Outsider* (London: Pan Books 1965), p 81.
6 Alfred North Whitehead, *Symbolism: Its Meaning and Effect* (New York: Capricorn Books 1927), p 21.
7 Whitehead, *Symbolism*, p 23.
8 Wilson, *Beyond the Outsider*, p 82.
9 Whitehead, *Symbolism*, p 44.
10 See Paul Colinvaux, *Introduction to Ecology* (New York: Wiley 1973), ch 28, for a good discussion of predatory control of prey species.
11 I am indebted to John Livingston for this suggestion.
12 Attributed to Gifford Pinchot. See Stephen Fox, 'Conservation: Past, Present, and Future,' in Neil Evernden, ed, *The Paradox of Environmentalism* (Toronto: York University 1984), p 22.
13 John Livingston, *The Fallacy of Wildlife Conservation*, (Toronto: McClelland & Stewart 1981).
14 Gregory Bateson, *Steps to an Ecology of Mind* (New York: Ballantine 1972), pp 443–4.

15 Marjorie Grene, *Approaches to a Philosophical Biology* (New York: Basic Books 1968), p 48.

16 Adolph Portmann, *New Paths in Biology* (New York: Harper & Row 1964), p 133.

17 Arthur Koestler, *The Ghost in the Machine* (London: Hutchinson 1967), p 166.

18 Grene, *Approaches*, p 149.

19 Grene, *Approaches*, pp 149–50.

20 Grene, *Approaches*, p 191.

21 Grene, *Approaches*, p 150.

22 Grene, *Approaches*, p 151.

23 F.J.J. Buytendijk, *Woman: A Contemporary View* (New York: Newman Press 1968), p 216.

24 Mary Midgley, *Beast and Man: The Roots of Human Nature* (New York: New American Library 1978), pp 18–19.

25 Martin Heidegger, *Being and Time* (New York: Harper & Row 1962), p 221.

26 Heidegger, *Being and Time*, pp 216–17.

27 Heidegger, *Being and Time*, p 232.

28 Heidegger, *Being and Time*, p 233.

28 Heidegger, *Being and Time*, p 234.

30 Adolph Portmann and Marjorie Grene, 'Beyond Darwinism,' *Commentary*, 40 (1965), 41.

31 See Paul Shepard, *Nature and Madness* (San Francisco: Sierra Club Books 1982).

32 M.H. Abrams, *Natural Supernaturalism: Tradition and Revolution in Romantic Literature* (New York: Norton 1971), p 267. The original reference is to a phrase in Coleridge's poem *Limbo*, which he subsequently used in reference to materialists in *The Friend*.

33 See Shepard, *Nature and Madness*.

34 Hans Jonas, *The Phenomenon of Life* (New York: Delta 1966), p 25.

CHAPTER SIX

1 Mary Douglas, 'Environments at Risk,' in Jonathan Benthall, ed, *Ecology: The Shaping Enquiry* (London: Longman 1972), p 139.

2 J.H. van den Berg, *The Changing Nature of Man* (New York: Delta 1961), p 231.

3 R. Rilke, cited in van den Berg, *Changing Nature of Man*, p 231.

4 Martin Heidegger, *Basic Writings*, ed David Krell (New York: Harper & Row 1977), p 296.

5 Gregory Bateson, *Steps to an Ecology of Mind* (New York: Ballantine 1972), p 433.

6 William Barrett, *Irrational Man* (New York: Anchor 1962), p 224.

7 Maurice Merleau-Ponty, *Phenomenology of Perception* (London: Routledge & Kegan Paul 1962), p 11.

8 Merleau-Ponty, *Phenomenology*, p 78.

9 R.D. Laing, *The Politics of Experience* (Harmondsworth: Penguin 1967), p 35.

10 Laing, *Politics*, p 36.

11 Laing, *Politics*, p 117.

12 Martin Buber, *I and Thou* (New York: Scribner's 1970), p 56.

13 Buber, *I and Thou*, p 78.

14 Buber, *I and Thou*, p 80.

15 Buber, *I and Thou*, p 67.

16 Harold F. Searles, *The Nonhuman Environment in Normal Development and in Schizophrenia* (New York: International Universities Press 1960), p 388.

17 Searles, *The Nonhuman Environment*, p 118.

18 M.H. Abrams, *Natural Supernaturalism: Tradition and Revolution in Romantic Literature* (New York: Norton 1971), p 344.

19 Abrams, *Natural Supernaturalism*, p 375.

20 Merleau-Ponty, *Phenomenology*, p xiii.

21 Merleau-Ponty, *Phenomenology*, p vii.

22 Linda Rosen Obst, 'Phenomenology Has a New Star, *New York Times*, Sunday, 26 November 1978.

23 Percy Bysshe Shelley, cited in Abrams, *Natural Supernaturalism*, p 384.

24 Abrams, *Natural Supernaturalism*, p 379.

25 Gaston Bachelard, *The Poetics of Space* (Boston: Beacon Press 1969), p 156.

26 José Ortega y Gasset, *Phenomenology and Art* (New York: Norton 1975), p 58.

27 Ortega, *Phenomenology and Art*, p 36.

28 Joseph Campbell, *The Masks of God: Creative Mythology* (New York: Viking 1968), pp 7–8.

29 Bachelard, *Poetics of Space*, p 106.

EPILOGUE

1 These figures come from a compilation reported by Charles Bergman in his extraordinary book *Wild Echoes: Encounters with the Most Endangered Animals in North America* (Anchorage: Alaska Northwest Books 1990).

2 Lest this seem to be simply a reference to innate 'instincts,' I must emphasize that the *Umwelt* refers to the sum total of the reality which constitutes the subject's world, whether that be influenced by physical limitations or by learning through experience. In the case in point, the dog certainly is capable of seeing the sparrow, but it has learned in infancy that the bird is not 'worth' noticing – that it can play no significant part in the dog's own life-world. See the discussion of Jakob von Uexküll and his concept of *Umwelt* above, p 82.

3 This 'ignorance' stems not from lack of learning, but from learning to ignore.

4 I have previously discussed this topic and its relevance to conservation, in my essay 'Ecology in Conservation and Conversation,' in Max Oelschlaeger, ed, *After Earth Day: Continuing the Conservation Effort* (Denton: University of North Texas Press 1992), pp 73–82. Obviously, organisms vary in the breadth of their dietary interests and therefore in their potential for interference with others, but I am speaking of the general tendency to segregate into distinct domains so as to minimize direct competition with other species.

5 Paul Colinvaux, *Introduction to Ecology* (New York: John Wiley & Sons 1973), p 342. For a highly readable version of Colinvaux's ecological insights, see his *Why Big Fierce Animals Are Rare* (Princeton: Princeton University Press 1978), particularly ch 13, 'Peaceful Coexistence.'

6 For details see Colinvaux, *Introduction to Ecology*, pp 343–4. His example, taken from the work of David Lack, dates from the 1930s. The recent response to the decimation of codfish populations off the Grand Banks of Newfoundland, however, demonstrates that little has changed: seals were promptly blamed for eating 'our' fish.

7 Colinvaux describes the human proclivity to niche-appropriation more bluntly in *Why Big Fierce Animals Are Rare* (p 238): 'As long as the finding of new ways in which to live was left to natural selection, there was always a tenuous peaceful coexistence of the living things on earth. But eventually one kind of animal found it possible to keep occupying new niches at will, always adding the niche-spaces of others to its own, escaping the ancient constraint of a fixed niche that is imposed on all others by natural selection. This animal yet continued to obey the other dictum of natural selection, which is to raise the largest possible number of off-

spring. The activities of this new form of animal are inevitably hostile to the interest of almost all the other kinds, for it engages in aggressive competition, instead of peaceful coexistence, in its drive for ever more young.'

8 Walker Percy, *Lost in the Cosmos: The Last Self-Help Book* (New York: Washington Square Books 1983), p 100.

9 George Steiner, *George Steiner: A Reader* (Oxford: Oxford University Press 1984), p 398.

10 In his interview in David Cayley's *The Age of Ecology* (Toronto: James Lorimer & Co. 1991), Wolfgang Sachs observes (p 117) that 'people talk too easily about the "environment." What was once a call for new public virtues is now about to be turned into a call for a new set of managerial strategies. When one sees how the World Bank begins to move into environment, when one sees how the experts of yesterday, the industrialists of yesterday, the planners of yesterday, without much hesitation, move into the field of the environment and declare themselves the caretakers of the world's environment, the suspicion grows that the experts of these institutions have now found a new arena to prove their own indispensability, and all in the name of ecology and the survival of the planet ... Now, with the alarm that the survival of the planet is in danger, we slowly move into a situation where there is no limit to intervention any more, because can you imagine any better justification for large-scale interventions in people's lives than the survival of the planet?'

11 Gifford Pinchot, *The Fight for Conservation* (Seattle: University of Washington Press 1967), p 45 (originally published in 1910).

12 Ibid, pp 79–80.

13 Fro Harlem Brundtland, *Our Common Future / World Commission on Environment and Development* (Oxford: Oxford University Press 1987), p 8.

14 I have discussed this convergence between Brundtland and Pinchot in a somewhat different context in 'Ecology in Conservation and Conversation.'

15 Pinchot, *The Fight for Conservation*, p 42.

16 Wolfgang Sachs, 'The Archaeology of the Development Idea,' *Interculture*, 109 (Fall 1990), 4.

17 See Stephen Fox, 'Conservation, Past, Present, and Future,' in Neil Evernden, ed, *The Paradox of Environmentalism* (Toronto: York University 1984), p 22.

18 Wolfgang Sachs, 'Archaeology of the Development Idea,' p 25.

19 Bergman, *Wild Echoes*, p 82.

20 Christopher Lasch, *The True and Only Heaven* (New York: Norton 1991), p 530.

21 Sachs, 'Archaeology of the Development Idea,' p 26.

22 The Brundtland Commission, cited by Sachs in 'Archaeology of the Development Idea' (p 25), in which he points out that the reframing of the indictment of growth as simply a problem of conservation – that is, of maintaining resources for continued 'development' – is what permits the Commission to speak from a position of apparent strength: environment is now part of the global economy. Furthermore, 'the global eco-system approach was successful only because it was wholly compatible with the interests of the development elite: it shared their perspective – the lofty heights of worldwide planning – and apprehended the confusion in the world neatly and tidily in clear sets of data that practically clamoured for action' (p 24).

23 Steiner, *George Steiner: A Reader*, p 398.

24 Sachs notes that there are roughly 5100 languages spoken on earth at the moment, only 1 per cent of which are European. But, he says, 'all indicators suggest that within a generation not many more than 100 of these languages will survive' ('Archeology of the Development Idea,' p 28).

25 Gregory Bateson's essay 'What Is an Instinct' in *Steps to an Ecology of Mind* (New York: Ballantine 1972), pp 38–58, begins thus:
Daughter: Daddy, what is an instinct?
Father: An instinct, my dear, is an explanatory principle.
D: But what does it explain?
F: Anything – almost anything at all. Anything you want to explain.
D: Don't be silly. It doesn't explain gravity.
F: No. But that is because nobody wants 'instinct' to explain gravity. If they did, it would explain it. We could simply say that the moon has an instinct whose strength varies inversely as the square of the distance ...

26 Even though this faith is beyond us, it is interesting that the sphere of faith – religion – has, by and large, been a source of limitation, of saying we may go 'this far but no farther.' The really novel thing about the modern religion of humanism is that it constitutes a faith in the *absence* of limits; indeed, even to suggest human limitations is blasphemy. This, no doubt, is one of the greatest impediments to the acquisition of a cultural equivalent of 'embodied limits.' On this, see David Ehrenfeld, *The Arrogance of Humanism* (New York: Oxford University Press 1978).

27 Henry Beston, *The Outermost House* (New York: Penguin 1988), p 25.

Index